2.2.

Luath Press Limited

committed to publishing well written books worth reading

LUATH PRESS takes its name from Robert Burns, whose little collie Luath (*Gael.*, swift or nimble) tripped up Jean Armour at a wedding and gave him the chance to speak to the woman who was to be his wife and the abiding love of his life. Burns called one of the 'Twa Dogs' Luath after Cuchullin's hunting dog in Ossian's *Fingal*. Luath Press was established in 1981 in the heart of Burns country, and is now based a few steps up the road from Burns' first lodgings on Edinburgh's Royal Mile. Luath offers you distinctive writing with a hint of unexpected pleasures.

Most bookshops in the UK, the US, Canada, Australia, New Zealand and parts of Europe, either carry our books in stock or can order them for you. To order direct from us, please send a £sterling cheque, postal order, international money order or your credit card details (number, address of cardholder and expiry date) to us at the address below. Please add post and packing as follows: UK – £1.00 per delivery address; overseas surface mail – £2.50 per delivery address; overseas airmail – £3.50 for the first book to each delivery address, plus £1.00 for each additional book by airmail to the same address. If your order is a gift, we will happily enclose your card or message at no extra charge.

Luath Press Limited
543/2 Castlehill
The Royal Mile
Edinburgh EH1 2ND
Scotland
Telephone: +44 (0)131 225 4326 (24 hours)
Email: sales@luath. co.uk
Website: www. luath.co.uk

THE SPORTS BUSINESS

THE
SPORTS BUSINESS
Neil Wilson

PIATKUS

First published in 1988
by Judy Piatkus (Publishers) Ltd,
5 Windmill Street, London W1P 1HF

British Library Cataloguing in Publication Data

Wilson, Neil, *1944 –*
    The sports business: the men and the money
    1. Sports. Sponsorship
    I. Title
    796′ .079

    ISBN 0-86188-727-1

Typeset in 11 on 13 pt Sabon by
Action Typesetting, Gloucester
Printed by Billing & Sons Ltd, Worcester

*To all those who helped
and those, at home,
who endured*

CONTENTS

INTRODUCTION

WHEN the downhill skier Bill Johnson became the first American to win the Olympic title in Sarajevo in 1984, his first thought was gold. Not the medal. The money. Asked what winning meant to him, he replied: 'Money, money, money. Millions.'

Since the swimmer, Mark Spitz, traded his seven Munich gold medals on Madison Avenue, Olympic gold has been a convertible currency, and striking gold is striking it rich. The queues now at the door are not autograph hunters but agents and advertisers and those who will turn fame into fortune. Those who still believe, as the founder of the modern Olympics proclaimed, that the most important thing is not to win but to take part, belong to another world. On her way to victory at the 1984 Games in Los Angeles, the marathon runner Joan Benoit actually ran past a huge advertising hoarding bearing her name and picture.

In only thirty years, during which time soccer, tennis, skiing and even the Olympics have abolished amateurism as a concept, sport has become unrecognizable from the games people once played. Millions of us, of course, still play for the fun of it, but we are not amateurs. We are just not good enough to be paid.

Money is the name of today's game, the price as important as the score. One golf shot has earned a million dollars. A woman brought up in a Communist country earned herself a million dollars just as a bonus, while a compatriot won a diamond-encrusted tennis racket. A rookie quarter-back entering the

National Football League in the USA, without the experience of a single professional game, has been offered more than one million dollars a year. Two boxers in America have split $25 million for one fight, and a runner has been paid $27,000 to sprint for ten seconds. A soccer club in Europe has spent more than £3 million buying the services of one player, and, in Britain, a jockey has gone to prison for defrauding the Inland Revenue of just as much.

Official figures in Britain estimate that more than $4 billion is spent on sport each year, more than on motor vehicles. In Britain, sport-related activity employs 376,000 people, more than the chemical industry, or agriculture or the combined electricity and gas industries. Sport is an industry. An American division of a British company which makes sports shoes predicts sales world-wide of more than $2 billion in 1989.

Major corporations pay huge sums in sponsorship to be associated with sport, and hardly anything moves on the games field without a name on it. At times sponsors appear to have their names in print as often in the sports pages as in the *Financial Times*. Spectator sport seems to have decided that it cannot survive without them.

Sport at the highest level is not recreation for the elite but a division of the entertainment industry. For show business, read the sports business. The dreams that came true in Hollywood in the thirties come true in the sports arenas today; instant fame, instant fortune, at the playing of a ball or the throwing of a punch.

It is television, not the cinema, that has transformed sport and the lives of all those who play it, organize it and promote it at the highest level. For the programme makers, and their audiences, sport is real-life soap opera. It has drama, excitement and an infinite variety of endings, and it can be brought to you in your living room from every corner of the globe at the instant it is happening – from the jungle in Kinshasa to a mountain top in the Rockies.

Only fifty years ago television flirted with sport when a few hundred viewers in London saw twenty-five minutes of action from a men's singles match at Wimbledon. But it was with the invention of the videotape and the advent of colour in the 1960s that sport and television began a serious affair which became today's marriage of convenience.

For the established sports, television offered greater income; for minority sports, it offered projection. Nothing was too much to ask of sports desperate to catch television's eye. Traditions, even rules, were tossed aside at the merest hint that by doing so they would please the one-eyed god they had come to worship. Cricket created new one-day competitions for it, and played in pink shirts with a yellow ball under floodlights. Tennis introduced the tie-breaker into its scoring system and moved Wimbledon's men's final to a Sunday. Golf dropped its random draw, and the International Olympic Committee moved the cycle of future Winter Olympics by two years. Squash even rebuilt its courts in glass and painted yellow stripes on its ball.

Pastimes redolent of drinking clubs, like darts and snooker, were transformed into professional sports by television. Occasionally, a sport was transplanted by television into a foreign land where there was no tradition for it, and took root.

Today, television influences everything to do with sport: who competes and what they wear, the day they play, the time, the place, the rules, the colour of the ball and, in American football, even the judges' decisions.

In return, competitive sport is given exposure beyond the dreams of those who created it as their recreation little more than a century ago. Who then could have conceived of an audience of two billion people for an Olympic Games?

Around that has grown the sports business, a nouveaux riche class of players, their agents, promoters, sponsors and equipment manufacturers, each dependent on the other and all dependent on television for spreading the gospel of sport.

All the people in this book are a part of that business. They have in common the fact that at least a million dollars has passed through their hands in one way or another. This was not a qualification to appear in the book but happens, coincidentally, to be the case. Some of them take not a penny of it for themselves. Some would not earn a penny themselves without it. All of them have helped to make sport what it is today, for better or worse.

The book itself is not seeking to be comprehensive. There are many influential people within sport who have made or controlled fortunes who will not be found within these pages. Those highlighted were chosen only because they and their roles are representative of the new generation of sport. One person I worked for, another I worked with, and several I have interviewed over the years as a sports journalist, and finding that the tracks of most of them had crossed was one of the fascinations.

Most have participated in sport at some level: Sebastian Coe and Dick Pound in the Olympics, Buzzer Hadingham in the French tennis championships, Frank Williams in Formula 3 racing, Mickey Duff in professional fights, Bob Woolf in college basketball and Barry Hearn in the London and New York marathons.

Sport's future growth as a major sector in the leisure industry, they agree, depends to a great extent on its relationship with television, particularly on the growth of competition, from the new satellite cable channels to the established networks and cartels such as the European Broadcasting Union. More than that, it depends on sport's attitude to television and which partner to the marriage wears the pants.

Duff and Hearn, men who have used television to promote their particular sports, would be happy for a trial separation, if not a divorce, believing that the time has come to exclude the medium from more events and encourage the return of the live audience. But that assumes that there is an audience still willing to drag itself away from its fireside, from its instant-action replays and informed commentaries, to halls and stadia which too often are antiquated, bleak and uncomfortable.

Television is responsible to a great degree for the growth of the sports business and the growth of sport itself. Sport also has it to thank for the modern sophistication of its audiences, who have money to spend but demand the best in return. For sport now to make any attempt to turn the clock back to a time before the invasion of the cameras into their world would not only be impossible but undesirable.

Modern communications, such as television, have shrunk the sporting world to little more than a village. The paths of those I interviewed had crossed frequently, and, while I was talking with them, Hearn and Duff were linked in the promotion of the heavyweight fight between Joe Bugner and Frank Bruno at White Hart Lane where Scholar was their landlord. Indeed, Bob Woolf showed me a handwritten note he had received from Mark

McCormack, another sporting agent, and commented on the re-markable similarity to his own. 'What would a handwriting expert make of that?' he asked. 'Perhaps what we do takes a certain type.'

I think it does. A sporting type. Because it was apparent to me that all had a fondness for sport which went far beyond their business and financial interests in it.

His Excellency Juan Antonio Samaranch, president of the International Olympic Committee and the inspiration for its more commercial approach.

1

THE GAMES

BY ONE of those splendid ironies, the sale of the Olympic ideal to the multi-national corporations of the West was announced a few hundred metres inside the Socialist bloc in East Berlin.

At last, five years into his presidency of the International Olympic Committee, Juan Antonio Samaranch, Spanish banker and businessman, had overcome the personal and political obstacles to the sporting sale of the century; the marketing of an ideal of perfection in the market places of capitalism.

The last of those obstacles, Monique Berlioux, the dominant executive director of the International Olympic Committee for seventeen years, had been dispatched with a golden handshake at a meeting in Berlin only a few hours earlier. She had stood in the way of swift progress, and had had to go, a victim of Samaranch's determination to run the Olympic movement in the future in the way he saw best.

Fundamental to that future was the marketing of the Olympic's five rings. When Samaranch succeeded to the presidency during the 1980 Olympic Games, the IOC was rich from the pickings of rights fees offered it by American television. In the previous decade, these had transformed it from an organization close to penury in 1968 to one whose legacy to Samaranch when he became president was a nest egg of more than $40 million.

What concerned Samaranch was his realization that this fiscal foundation was wholly dependent on the quadrennial fix from the US TV networks, something brought home to him by the effects of the boycott of the 1980 Games in Moscow by the United States and its allies, and the millions the IOC lost in television rights. If he was to ensure that no country had the ability to hold the Olympics to ransom in that way again, the IOC needed to become more independent by becoming less dependent. Diversify, he had urged the IOC, and his announcement in Berlin that, for the first time, it was willing to sell the five rings for commercial gain was his most significant move towards diluting the power of television.

The Commission for New Sources of Finance (CNSF) had been established within the IOC before Samaranch's presidency but only at his enthusiastic prompting did it actively pursue its objectives. The sale of Olympic stamps, coins and publications were all considered, and all put aside because of their limitations. It needed a bolder stroke.

In the normal course of his journeying around the sporting world, Samaranch's path crossed that of Horst Dassler, son of the founder of the Adidas sportswear empire who, since his father's death, controlled the day-to-day running of one of the world's larger private companies. Dassler maintained close links with leading sports officials of all countries, some said a closeness unhealthy for the independence of sporting organizations, but it made him the perfect adviser to Samaranch. He understood both the business of selling and the politics of sport.

He had another pertinent experience. In the seventies he had created a company in Monaco, with the British marketing agent Patrick Nally (see chapter 10), which had marketed the rights of the Fédération Internationale de Football Associations (FIFA) and its World Cup. These rights had been taken over in 1982 by two new inter-dependent companies, based in Lucerne in Switzerland, which Dassler formed under the presidency of his former personal assistant at Adidas, Klaus Hempel. They were called ISL Marketing and ISL Licensing.

Dassler warned Samaranch that it would not be easy. He told him of the time-consuming negotiations which had had to be conducted with each of the major national associations in soccer before FIFA's programme could be put together, and the enormous sums of money which the Coca-Cola Company had had to pay out on FIFA's behalf initially to buy back rights to their own product in some countries. But he offered ISL's services to undertake an investigation into the possibility of the IOC taking the international marketing of the Olympics under its own control.

In March, 1983, ISL made its first report to CNSF, suggesting a marketing programme jointly benefiting the IOC and the National Olympic Committees (NOCs) of every country. It had Samaranch's official stamp of approval and the CNSF commissioned further market research and more detailed proposals.

Berlioux was not opposed in principle. Indeed, she was a hardworking supporter of all schemes which would increase the standing and influence of the IOC. None had worked harder for it during the presidencies of Samaranch's predecessors, the American Avery Brundage and the Irish peer Lord Killanin. What her critics believed concerned her was the diminution of her own power and influence, and she felt a natural antipathy towards the direct involvement of any outside agency, such as ISL, and particularly one controlled by a man as powerful as Dassler.

Berlioux, a former Olympic swimmer for France, who had joined the IOC first as a press officer in 1967, had come to control the organization in the absence from Lausanne of Brundage and Killanin, who both preferred to work from their homes in Chicago and Dublin respectively. Samaranch, a banker and businessman who had been Spain's ambassador to the Soviet Union in the four years before becoming IOC president, saw his role differently.

Within weeks of the end of the Moscow Games, he had moved into residence in a suite at the sumptuous and elegant Palace Hotel in Lausanne. Soon Berlioux's secretariat on one floor of Chateau de Vidy, the former manor house which was the IOC's headquarters, was matched by Samaranch's own on another floor. Each had its own staff, mutually suspicious and loyal to their own leader. There was a fight even over the positioning of the IOC's telex machine because of the access it gave to information, and several staff Berlioux saw as disloyal to her left. 'She probably had something to do with the high turnover of personnel,' suggested Killanin in his autobiography.

At one dinner she shared with the president during the first few months of their partnership, she enquired of him how much longer he would be living in Lausanne. 'I don't think there is room in this city for both of us,' she said frankly and, as it turned out, prophetically.

Samaranch did not choose the Olympic marketing operation as the killing ground but it was so important to him that Berlioux's unwillingness to countenance ISL's involvement as anything more than consultants was slowing progress.

By late 1984, ISL's proposals had been refined but they were hardly any further down the road to their implementation. They seemed to be getting contrasting feedback from within the IOC, and were constantly having to seek more time to make more changes. Finally, with the next four-year Olympic cycle before 1988 beginning, Samaranch's patience ran out. He turned to one of his trusted lieutenants, Dick Pound, a Canadian tax attorney newly elected in 1983 to the IOC's executive board, the inner cabinet.

'Deek, you do it,' Pound remembers him saying, mimicking the Catalonian accent. Pound was appointed as an ad-hoc, ex-officio representative of the executive on the CNSF; 'the fix-it', in Pound's words.

'It was obvious to me that Berlioux was wrecking the programme by the position she was taking,' says Pound, like her, a former Olympic swimmer. 'She wanted ISL to be consultants only, so that every time they had got a deal together they would have to go down on their knees and present it to her for approval. It was insane, unworkable.'

In March, 1985, Pound met with ISL's executive vice-president, Jurgen Lens, in Calgary, the venue of the 1988 Winter Olympic. Lens said that ISL could not proceed further unless they had the power to act as the IOC's agents. Pound promised it to him. 'It took about seven seconds to resolve that log jam,' he says. Within a month ISL had negotiated a contract between the IOC, the organizing committees of the two Games of 1988 and the United States Olympic Committee (USOC), whose area of responsibility made them crucial to the success of a marketing programme. It was announced in East Berlin.

Berlioux had arrived there, for the IOC Congress, unaware that her days were numbered. When a British journalist asked her whether she was about to leave the IOC, he was dismissed imperiously. Within twenty-four hours she was seeking him out to discover the source of his intelligence. Before she left Berlin she had resigned.

During her reign – which is how many of the IOC members saw her seventeen years in office – the IOC had grown out of all recognition. At the end of the Second World War it was without resources, beyond the subscriptions paid by its wealthy and privileged members, and the occasional private donation and legacy. Its expenditure exceeded its income in both 1946 and 1947 and in 1948 it passed a motion demanding a payment of £2,000 from the organizers of that year's Winter Games in St Moritz and £5,000 from those of the Summer Games in London.

Since 1922, during the lifetime of the modern Games' founder, Pierre de Coubertin, the headquarters of the most important organization in world sport had been a single floor of a former manor house. After 1946, when Otto Mayer became the first IOC Chancellor, he ran its affairs from a backroom of his family's exclusive jewellery shop in Lausanne and the bar of the next-door hotel, with only the help of a part-time secretary, Madame Lydia Zanchi, a lady of Russian origin.

Members, each elected for life by other members, had to pay their own travel and accommodation expenses as well as a subscription. Most were more than able to afford it. At the time Killanin became a member (he was the IOC's sixth peer) there were, in membership, one head of state, three princes, one archduke, three counts, three knights, a pasha, a rajah and several others entitled to the prefix honourable or excellency.

When Berlioux joined the IOC staff in 1967 there was little enough in the kitty to pay her salary. Television, with, as Lord Thompson once said, 'its licence to print money', changed everything.

An American TV network paid for the right to cover an Olympics for the first time in 1960 when CBS gave a total of $440,000 to the organizers of the Winter and Summer Games for the rights to screen thirty-five hours. But none of it came to the IOC, and nor did it again when the ABC network bought the US rights to the 1964 Winter Games and NBC bought rights to that year's Summer Games. Even when ABC paid $4 million for the Summer Games in Mexico, the $150,000 the organizers gave to the IOC was an ex-gratia payment not demanded by the IOC's own rules.

Only after those rules were changed did the IOC escape from penury, but by that time, in the years leading up to the Games in Sapporo and Munich, it was so hard up that it was living frugally off money borrowed against its share of the promised TV rights of DM43 million ($14 million). When Killanin succeeded Brundage towards the end of that year, there was $2,084,290 in the kitty after the disbursement of all debts. Eight years later when he handed on the presidency to Samaranch, the bottom line was $45,142,752 and 21 cents.

The Games of 1972 established television, and particularly American television, as the Olympic's milch-cow, and the competition between the three US networks drove the yield higher with each succeeding Games. Four years after Munich, ABC's fee had doubled and for Moscow, NBC offered more than double again; what seemed then to be an astonishing $87 million. In 1984, when ABC regained the rights, that figure was exceeded even by the fee of $91.5 million which it paid for the Winter Games and was dwarfed by its £225 million bid for the Summer Games in Los Angeles. But it was the experience of Moscow which had brought home to Samaranch the Olympic movement's dependence on TV.

NBC had caught a cold. Unable to screen the Games because of its government's decision to boycott the Moscow Games in protest at the Soviet invasion of Afghanistan, NBC, even after collecting on insurances, had been chilled by a $34 million loss. What would happen, asked Samaranch, if future Games were wrecked similarly by boycotts, a possibility ABC took care to guard themselves against by inserting a clause in its 1984 contract which ensured that it would be compensated if the United States team did not compete. Similarly, what would happen if anti-trust laws in American were changed to exclude the three TV networks and allow them to collude over fees?

It was a possibility which was highlighted by what happened over the TV negotiations for the 1988 Olympics, a tale of two cities which led to very different endings.

Calgary went in to bat first. They were advised by Trans World International, the television arm of sporting entrepreneur Mark McCormack's International Management Group. Following the conventional theory of negotiating they believed that the longer they delayed the more valuable their product.

The IOC's executive board saw it differently. It reasoned that ABC had paid an excessive fee for the 1984 Winter Games in Sarajevo because of the public interest generated by the US ice hockey team's victory in the 1980 Games. Would ABC be as interested in 1988, it asked, if the US team failed to do it again in 1984? It advised Calgary to do their deal before Sarajevo.

The IOC could not insist on it because it did not have the power under the terms of its contract with the Calgary organizers (a power it has since written into its contracts with the organizers of the 1992 Games). So it made IMG an offer: if they delayed until after the 1984 Games and the best they could negotiate was less than $200 million, IMG would pay the IOC the difference. IMG and the Calgary organizing committee declined to back their judgement, so the IOC insisted that negotiations should take place one month before the Sarajevo Games. Events proved their wisdom.

Each American network was sent a contract identical in every detail, with only the price left blank. Each had to sign it and return it to Pound *before* it could enter the bidding. 'It was that which led to the extraordinary result,' says Pound.

It helped, too, that the television market was buoyant and two of the personalities of the networks, Roone Arledge, ABC's president of news and sport, and Bob Mulholland, of NBC, wanted to be king of the mountains. 'They were in a Gunfight at OK Corral routine,' according to Pound.

The sealed bid brought offers of $250 million from CBS, $300m from NBC and $301 million from ABC, which had calculated correctly the likely round-figure bid of NBC. All three were vastly more than the IOC – or IMG – had expected, and they were unwilling to separate the two by the $1 million difference in their blind bids.

So a second round of bidding to break the deadline was imposed, with one important new rule. There would be a bid every fifteen minutes, and each bid had to be at least $1 million more than the last. NBC won the right to bid first by the toss of a coin, and then bid $304 million. ABC came back fifteen minutes later and said, in poker parlance, 'we shall see your four and raise you five' to $309 million. NBC folded their hand. 'It's yours,' said Mulholland to Arledge.

It was a victory he was to regret very quickly. The television market collapsed, the major networks were forced into major staff redundancies and within two years ABC was talking publicly of a possible loss of $70 million on its coverage, an estimate more recently reduced to $50 million by a damage control operation which trimmed its production costs in Calgary.

The 'extraordinary result' led, indirectly, to the disaster that was to follow for the organizers of the Summer Games in Seoul. Their expectations were raised by Calgary's success but in the intervening twenty months the networks had come to realize that too much had been paid for Calgary. ABC itself had even changed hands, coming under the control of more cost-conscious Capital Cities Communications.

So the Koreans came expecting not less than $600 million. 'We will take a very hard line with the networks – $600 million and not less,' said Lee Yong Ho, the country's Minister of Sport. Barry Frank, senior vice-president of TWI, who were agents for Seoul as they had been for Calgary, predicted immediately before the Sarajevo Games that they would get $700 million.

Imagine the shock then when negotiating opened in the Palace Hotel in Lausanne with CBS bidding $301 million, ABC $305 and NBC $325. 'It was a big loss of face for the Koreans,' says Pound, who as chairman of their television commission was the IOC's representative at the talks. 'They could not believe it.' Pound himself, who had been talking with the networks weekly, was stunned. He had said privately to the networks before the negotiations that 'we need a figure beginning with five', but they had never committed themselves.

Seoul's negotiators could not respond. They had a mandate to achieve at least $500 million, and they had to sit on their hands until it was morning again in Korea before they could get instructions from home. Samaranch himself called Rho Tae Woo, chairman of South Korea's ruling Democratic Party, to warn him that the networks were serious and that he should take what was offered, while Pound tried to convince the Koreans in Lausanne that it was a market offer and not an insult.

There was a photograph at the time in the American magazine *Sports Illustrated* showing Pound in discussion with Yong Ho, with three fingers raised. 'I was saying ... "third thing is that every hour we sit here with our thumbs up our asses it is costing us $10 million dollars",' recalled Pound.

Yong Ho replied that he knew better about negotiating with Americans. 'I spend six months of the year in America,' he told Pound. 'They will be back.' After nineteen hours of negotiating he went home empty-handed, the sides as far apart as ever. 'The problem with local organizing committees is that they always want the last dollar,' said Samaranch. 'They don't care whether they have good relations with the networks but we have to go on to the next Olympics, and the next.'

The IOC had no way to break the deadlock. Their agreement with the South Koreans was for joint negotiations. They were equal partners with neither having a casting vote. Before the sides met again the IOC privately urged the networks to make better offers; but all refused. CBS offered the same again and ABC were not going to make an offer until Pound begged Arledge to make a gesture, if only to convince NBC that they were still in the running. Arledge threw his original offer back into the ring.

NBC realized they were on their own. They dropped their offer by $25 million and the Koreans were forced to shake hands on a deal which gave them a minimum of $300 million and a maximum of $500 million. The difference was to be determined by 'gross adjusted advertising sales', the extra income which might be generated by Olympic coverage over and above normal advertising revenue for the period, but it was a device to save Korean faces. The Americans did not expect to pay one cent more than $300 million. 'It was a hideous disaster,' says Pound.

NBC knew they were in the driving seat. For the next six months their corporate men, some even from RCA, the parent company, took over from the sports department executives to negotiate the detailed contract line by line, making many demands the SLOC had to accede to and some which the IOC could never accept. In the beginning, the Korean government had agreed to the introduction of daylight saving to keep the time with the US east coast to fourteen hours and to move the Games forward seven days to avoid baseball's World Series. Later its organizing committee also had to make changes in the timetable to suit NBC. 'It was a most disagreeable process,' says Pound.

The effect of it will be evident when the networks bid for the

1992 Games in Albertville and Barcelona. Then, for the first time, the IOC has taken for itself the power to make the decisions, with the two organizing committees only being 'consulted' about the details. It does not expect the networks to agree to an 'identical contract' before the bidding, as they did for Calgary, but it does want ninety per cent of the detail agreed before the financial talking. 'We don't want to have to go through the Seoul experience again,' says Pound.

It is unlikely that the networks will ever again offer the fees they did for the Games of 1988. The US TV viewer is more selective now in his viewing. The best sporting events get audiences as high as ever. The Chicago Bears v. Miami Dolphins National Football League game in 1985 had the highest ratings ever. Generally, however, the ratings of even national obsessions, like football, are down, while production costs are up and advertisers have become more choosy, forcing rates down by buying at a discount at the last minute rather than a season in advance, as they used to.

The IOC claims it will not be too upset if the upward curve in the graph of American television income peaked in 1988. The more it is offered, the harder it is to refuse television anything. Pound denies that the IOC's judgement has been affected. 'The Olympic family get slightly less than twenty-five per cent of the total, so the temptations for us are a lot less than it would seem on paper,' he says.

Pound has personal experience of the power of the modern Olympics to corrupt. He is a tax attorney in Montreal, the city which will still be paying for the 1976 Games in the year 2000. Pound himself had a client who was a crane operator who was paid $120,000 for the hire of a crane, by the constructors of the Olympic Stadium, which they never used. The Montreal *Star* later calculated that the thirty-three cranes hired cost $1 million more than it would have cost to buy them.

Those Games were despoiled by those greedy for power, glory and money, and a watershed in Olympic extravagance. The final bill was $2,310 million. Pound sees no analogy with the IOC's recent commercialism even though he accepts that there were powerful commercial motivations for the IOC's decision to change the Olympic cycle from 1994 to keep the Winter and Summer Games two years apart.

ISL admit that few companies are willing to think as far ahead as four years in marketing terms, and television is delighted that it can spread its costs beyond a single year. And while the Swiss newspaper *Sport* said the decision was 'against the philosophy of Pierre de Coubertin (the Olympic founder)', Pound argues that staging the Olympics every two years also makes sporting sense.

What may harden after the Seoul experience is the IOC's attitude towards other parts of the world. In the past, the US networks have subsidized other TV companies as the IOC have sacrificed rights fees elsewhere to widen their audience (estimated at 2 billion world-wide in 1984). For the Los Angeles Games ABC were paying $1.67 per TV household compared with Europe's 17 cents. 'There is always a great shredding of clothing and pouring on of ashes, quite a polished performance of how it is not possible for them to pay anything,' says Pound of the negotiations with the European Broadcasting Union.

For the Calgary Games, Europe paid only $5.7 million. Considering that the major winter sports nations are in that continent it was an insulting fee compared to ABC's $309 million. Even for Seoul, Europe has paid only $9 million more than the $19 million it paid for Los Angeles, and little more than half what Japan has paid. Britain's share of the European offer will be less than one Australian station will pay.

Soon there will be alternatives to the European Broadcasting Union; cable, satellite channels and commercial companies, like Italy's Channel Five, whose counter offer forced up EBU's offer for Los Angeles, and France's Canal 4. Or the IOC may offer the European commercial companies, like ITV, the Games free in return for advertising during the Olympic transmissions for their commercial sponsors. 'Legislation may be required in some countries but it is a myth that there is no money in European television,' says Pound. 'They are a nine billion dollar industry. They can afford their share.'

Since Montreal in 1976, the Olympic Games have become increasingly dependent on television money. ABC paid forty-five per cent of the cost of Los Angeles staging their Games. NBC are still the second largest contributor to the Seoul Games after the South Korean government, while corporate sponsors will contribute little more than five per cent.

But Samaranch is convinced that if he is to achieve his ambition of leaving the Olympic movement as a powerful force for good in the world and economically independent of politics, it is in this area that the future lies. It was something else brought home to him by the experience of 1980 when those countries in the West which stood out against government calls for boycott, such as Britain, were those financially independent of their governments.

Even the mighty USOC were vulnerable that year. Their income came largely from tax deductible donations, and had they disagreed with their government's moral argument, they could not have withstood the economic persuasion of an unsympathetic US President able to remove the tax advantages.

The problem which the IOC dumped into ISL's lap was complex. Rule 53 of the Olympic Charter gave the exclusive right to use all Olympic names and symbols to each national Olympic Committee within its own territory.

So the IOC had no power to license its famous five rings anywhere and nor could Games' organizing committees sell their mascots and symbols for use outside their own country. So, world-wide marketing programmes had been impractical and most sponsorships had been local in nature.

The IOC knew that their own members would not vote to scrap a rule so beneficial to their own NOCs. The alternative, suggested ISL, was to make each a cash offer they could not refuse for the return of their rights under Rule 53. Pound doubted it would be possible. 'It was an enormous undertaking,' he says. Samaranch warned ISL – and Dassler – that they would be on their own. 'The IOC will not apply pressure on NOCs to accept,' he said.

'I thought they would do well to persuade 100 NOCs,' says Pound. Instead they persuaded 150 within eighteen months, including all those in the countries critical to a marketing operation.

There had been criticism of Samaranch and the executive board for awarding the deal to Dassler's ISL without inviting any other marketing agencies to tender. But it was precisely because ISL could use Adidas' contacts in NOCs and sporting federations in all the major countries that made them so useful to the IOC. 'I still don't believe that without Adidas' support on the ground in all these countries, it would have been possible,' says Pound.

The USOC were on board from the start, a partner to the agreement with ISL but too proud of its strength to admit within its own territory that it was part of a global IOC operation. NOCs in less developed markets which had no history of raising money for themselves were a push-over, happy for any handout. Hong Kong, tiny but with a strong business community, had to be compensated with a larger than average fee.

Even some socialist giants of the Olympic movement, most friendly with Dassler and contracted to Adidas for clothing for their national teams, embraced the idea wholeheartedly. The Soviet Union, who signed with ISL in November 1986, even organized a seminar in Moscow at which ISL were able to explain the project to twenty-six other countries, including all those from the Socialist bloc.

It was in NOCs in countries such as Britain and West Germany where ISL found their toughest opponents. These had marketed the Olympics in their own countries successfully since 1976. The British Olympic Association (BOA) made a net £475,762 towards its administrative expenses and the cost of transporting its team to the Games in 1976, using the services of a professional marketing agency. Four years later, after taking a professional fund-raiser, George Nicholson, onto its staff full-time, its income rose to £856,301, in spite of the emotions aroused by the government's call for a boycott. In 1984, Nicholson master-minded an operation which yielded a staggering £3.3 million before tax.

Nicholson took a lot of persuading that ISL had anything to offer him. He was a decade ahead of them in realizing the potential of sponsors. Multi-nationals, such as American Express, were helping Britain before ISL came on the scene, and ISL were given short shrift when they offered a single fee to buy-out all the BOA's rights in the forty-four categories of products that ISL had identified as worth selling world-wide.

Instead, Nicholson insisted that he would negotiate the 'sale' of each category separately. 'We haggled long and hard over each and I don't think I'd win any popularity poll at ISL,' says Nicholson, a former fund-raiser for the British charity Shelter which assists the homeless.

Nicholson squeezed almost $1 million from ISL, more than

fifty per cent of all he was to raise from sponsorship as part of a British appeal that would raise at least as much as in 1984. In a product category like credit cards, which he had sold well to American Express in 1984, he extracted a 'scandalously' high price because, he says, he had to justify the disloyalty to past supporters. Some products, like toiletries and cosmetics, which he had been able to sell on previous occasions within Britain, ISL failed to sell internationally. Most of the others, he claims, would have been easy to sell to sponsors in Britain because ISL were taking only the most sought-after categories 'But I'm grateful to ISL. We made more because of them.'

ISL could do nothing to clear the decks for sponsors in some markets because they had not been able to start work soon enough. Kodak have packaged their film world-wide with the Olympic rings, but have had to re-package it for the tiny Belgium market. That NOC already had an independent deal with another film company.

There were other problems for ISL associated with breaking new ground. When they put together the list of forty-four potential product categories in 1984 they had not had the experience of the sporting market-place they were to gain selling soccer's 1986 World Cup. It was a finger-in-the-wind exercise in which they sat around the table with the various Olympic factions trying to calculate a target figure.

Seoul would say they needed $3 million for rights to cameras, Calgary a million and the USOC a million and a half. ISL's figure was an aggregate, hardly a scientific way of arriving at a market value. Some were hopelessly unrealistic and were to cause internal tensions between the factions which ISL could have done without.

Then, when ISL made presentations to potential sponsors, many did not believe they could deliver the world-wide co-operation of NOCs, and some thought the lead-in time of little more than two years too short to be effective.

There were others, such as IBM and Xerox, who were only interested in about twenty of the 167 markets ISL were offering, and tried to persuade them to break up the programme into smaller, cheaper groups. Breweries and car makers were also not interested because their products are not sold under single global names.

Some, like American Express, thought that because they had no realistic rival globally they could bring the price down by delaying and were furious when VISA managed to gather its 16,000 client banks together to become involved.

Curiously, the Japanese market, which ISL had expected much of because of its proximity to Seoul, was never rewarding; possibly because of the weakness of the dollar against the yen, and only two of their companies bought into The Olympic Programme (TOP). Europe showed even less interest. Only the Dutch electronics giant Philips signed up, and even they did so at a lower than expected figure after several false starts and the collapse of one mega-deal.

In the end TOP was sold in only twenty-eight categories to nine companies: Coca-Cola, VISA, 3M, Brother, Philips, Federal Express, Kodak, Time Inc. and Panasonic, for a grand total of little more than $100 million. 'Not perfectly satisfactory but good enough first time round,' says Pound.

There was, of course, the spin-off for the Olympic movement of massive exposure for their name and image around the world. 3M estimate that they are spending fifty-five per cent of their total promotional budget during the period on their Olympic involvement. 'Future organizing committees will need to spend less time and money promoting their Games because it will be done for them,' says Pound.

What pleased the IOC was ISL's research in major markets. That showed that companies are less interested in involvements with particular Games than with an association with the Olympic image personified by the IOC's own five rings. In the United States, only the symbol of the fast food chain McDonald's was more recognizable, and then only by 100% against 99%.

'Essentially we are selling the good, clean Corinthian image of the Olympic Games,' says Andrew Craig, the ISL executive responsible for TOP. Not surprisingly, cigarette or pharmaceutical companies are on the IOC's banned list and so is any marketing presence within the arena.

Perversely, ISL are going to the same clients to sell soccer and the Olympics but with different packages. The most saleable element of any soccer package are the advertising boards within the arenas at FIFA's World Cup finals. Yet the IOC package does not offer any advertising boards. Indeed, since the 1984 Games when the sky above the Olympic stadium was full of advertising balloons, Rule 53 has been amended to ban advertising even in the sky above arenas.

Craig does not find anything contrary about the differences. 'We are not selling image with soccer. Involvement with vast numbers of people, yes, and tremendous exposure, but our research found that with the Olympics, association was what was important. Almost half of all the people interviewed in samples in the United States, Singapore, Portugal and West Germany thought that the Olympic rings would indicate that the product was of good quality.'

Putting advertising in the Olympic arena might, thinks Craig, have an adverse effect on the image. 'It is probably the only sporting event apart from Wimbledon which is not cluttered with advertising,' he says. 'In people's minds that is a mark of its high quality and importance. What we might gain from selling boards we might lose in the quality of our image.' As Pound says, 'What sets the Olympic apart is that you can always see the athletes in our arena.'

Even so the TOP clients will be conspicuously present at Olympic Games. Their contracts entitle them to large numbers of tickets, and acres of hotel space have been blocked off for their personnel and guests in the Olympic cities. Hoteliers predict that the magnificent dinner for 700 which Dassler gave in Seoul to trumpet ISL's cause will pale beside the junketing planned by the TOP sponsors.

All nine have taken hoardings around the Olympic venues to project their involvement, and the road from Calgary's International Airport into the city were an avenue of advertising. Philips were so anxious to keep in with all sides that during the bidding for the 1992 Olympic site they pledged their support on hoardings in both Amsterdam and Barcelona.

They are not alone. Each organizing committee has its own smaller, national sponsors. A year before their Games, the South Korean Olympic Organising Committee had signed up ninety-seven Korean companies and the income from sponsorship, supply and licensed deals already then exceeded $150 million, $15 million more than the hugely profitable Los Angeles Games made from marketing.

None of the nine TOP sponsors is guaranteed a renewal of their contracts for another four years. IOC rules prevent any commercialization until after the closing ceremony of the previous Games. Even ISL, who had to make a considerable financial guarantee to the IOC and USOC in their first contract, cannot sign a new contract with the IOC until after January of 1989, although Dassler was promised before he died in 1987 that they would not have to go out to tender for it.

TOP sponsors do not have a clause giving them an option or first refusal on the next four years but the IOC promises to discuss it first with them. 'We shall think highly of those who supported us the first time,' says Pound diplomatically, knowing that while one paid as much as $14 million some paid less than the market rate as a toe-dipping exercise.

He expects other larger fish who did not bite first time to be tempted by the bait next time. IBM turned down a TOP deal for computers originally, but later signed a deal directly with Seoul. ISL believe that there are many more who 'fit' perfectly into TOP, just as Federal Express, a company well known in the US and keen to be better known elsewhere, did.

It would also not be surprising if one or two of the present nine do not want to come back. Time Inc., who bought the publications category for *Time*, *Sports Illustrated* and *Asiaweek,* gained some adverse publicity with allegations of censorship when, on *Time*'s behalf, the Calgary organizing committee sought powers in the courts to prevent Canada's own national news magazine *Maclean*'s from bringing out a special Olympic souvenir edition.

'There's a lot of good faith involved and I think our present sponsors will say that we have been fair and reasonable with them,' says Pound. 'We've been around 100 years and we shall be for another 100, so we're not what you might call fly-by-nights.'

The resources so far generated have transformed the IOC. There is no figure available for their overall income but it is certain that at least $250 million has passed through their Swiss bank account since Samaranch became president.

The effects have been felt in every country. Their own headquarters have been expanded and modernized, and an Olympic museum has been built in Lausanne. The NOCs are now invited to send representatives to meetings at the IOC's expense, and the

IOC pay for a proportion of the athletes each country sends to a Games. Olympic Solidarity, an organization within the IOC created to develop sport in the Third World, has a budget now of around $30 million and it underwrites everything from coaching courses to sports constructions.

The IOC has also looked after its own. No longer do their members pay their own way. Members travel first class on the IOC to its congresses and live like the lords many still are, but it is hardly an unreasonable recompense for the unpaid work some do. Pound reckons that as an executive board member and a commission chairman he spends at least 1,000 hours every year – more than 100 working days – on unpaid work for the organization, and he charges nothing for his considerable experience as a qualified lawyer and accountant when he checks through every commercial contract the IOC sign. His law practice earns nothing in return. So that he is not seen to be benefiting from the IOC, the law firm in which he is a partner does none of the IOC's legal work.

Samaranch himself works full-time as president, and could not have done more to achieve all he has in his first eight years of office. He resigned as the Spanish ambassador to the Soviet Union before he began as IOC President and, while he keeps a home in his native land, he is more often in Lausanne or travelling on IOC business.

He was not a great sportsman himself, although he was a useful roller hockey player in a country where the sport is popular and he cut his administrative teeth helping the sport out as an honorary administrator. 'He is not a great ideas man but when he gets hold of anything he gets things done,' says a fellow Catalan sports official.

'He is a great listener,' says Pound. 'For the time you are with him you feel you are the most important thing in his world. But he uses his time very efficiently. He seems to be able to get things done in fifteen-minute cycles.'

The IOC now has its own presidential plane and Samaranch, a dapper and sprightly sixty-eight, has visited more than 100 of the member countries. It is in that almost Papal role, handshaking and waving, that he is perceived publicly; but it is as a skilled diplomat and politician that he has steered the Olympics away from the rough waters of controversy which were surrounding them.

One Swiss newspaper dubbed him the 'The Great Restorer' for pushing through more radical changes in his years than previous presidents had in sixty years. Indeed, he has been the Olympic's Thatcher, pulling the movement out of its inflationary spiral and introducing private enterprise into a monolith which had become dependent on a public prop. 'Ignoring building, you can organize a good Olympics again for $500 million and not leave any debts,' says Pound. That alone would be a priceless legacy for Samaranch to leave from his presidency.

Buzzer Hadingham, chairman of the All England Lawn Tennis and Croquet Club since 1983.

2

The championship

THE ALL-ENGLAND Lawn Tennis and Croquet Club is not a company within the terms of the Companies Act or even a fund-raising operation recognized by the Charity Commissioners. It is a private club without shareholders, directors or dividends to pay. Indeed, within the club, it is not thought proper to regard what appears on the bottom line as profit but rather, as its chairman says, a surplus of income over expenditure.

Yet, when the counting was completed in the autumn of 1987, the year's accounts of the activities of a club with 375 members paying an annual subscription of only £30 showed that surplus to be somewhere in the order of £7 million.

Nobody on the club's committee had done their sums wrong, or robbed a bank. The explanation was more prosaic. The club's annual tennis tournament, popularly known as Wimbledon, had again worked its magic.

On an autumn day, it is hard to imagine that each summer this tranquil place in the south-west of London is taken over by one of the world's most renowned sporting occasions. With the nets and posts and green canvas removed the courts that resounded to the volleys of Lendl and Becker in June are lawn again, and the only activity apparent is the gentler movement of four lady members playing a doubles game on a hard court.

Yet behind the Virginia creeper which adorns the walls of the club's offices, a commercial operation goes on which takes no account of the seasons. A club which, legend has it, first organized a championship to fund the purchase of a new roller, has transformed a piece of Victoriana into a business enterprise which is the wonder and envy of the sporting world. Today, the playing of tennis by the world's finest players is only one part of the club's trading activities.

Final confirmation of the metamorphosis was the decision of the club's committee in 1986 to end its custom of making public the minutiae of its income and expenditure accounts. It was, said RHE 'Buzzer' Hadingham, CBE, chairman of the committee of management, in deference to the needs for 'commercial confidentiality of our customers'. He was not speaking of the thousands of paying spectators who flock to the club's grounds in the last two weeks of June, but of the multi-national corporations and television networks with whom the club does business the year round.

In 1983, another decision minuted by the committee reveals the importance it was attaching to its non-playing activities. After more than a century, the club recognized that the traditional title of 'secretary' was no longer appropriate to the man fronting its commercial operation, Christopher Gorringe. He had been secretary since 1979 and assistant secretary for six years before that but in future he was to be known as Chief Executive. Subsequently, marketing, financial and championship directors were appointed to support him.

Yet, for all this full-time expertise that was brought to bear on the club's affairs, the corporate decisions were being taken in the same way they had been for one hundred years by a committee of twelve chosen by fellow members at the annual meeting of a private and very exclusive club which for the best part of a century had been a bastion of amateurism.

The members are not all archetypes of the English establishment, unlike perhaps their early predecessors. True, there is a peer of the realm and was, until 1987, a former Home Secretary but the first is known to all as Hugo and dares sit on the media sub-committee, and the other's more appropriate former position was in the umpire's seat for a Wimbledon final.

Among the other members are individuals whom any major corporation would be pleased to have on their board: a former chief executive of the Milk Marketing Board, the chairman and chief executive of an international electronics company, a senior partner in a law firm, an accountant, several Varsity Blues and six former players in The Championships with the former champion Virginia Wade amongst them. The average age is an unstuffy fifty-four. 'All people with a love of the game and no axes to grind,' as Gorringe puts it. Nothing is more certain to get Hadingham's dander up than expressing surprise that such a committee could run a commercial enterprise dealing with contracts worth millions. 'It infuriates me to hear people say that Wimbledon is run by amateurs,' he says. 'We are honorary and we are part-time, but we are not amateurs.'

Hadingham himself is as steeped in the commercial world as he is in tennis. He worked for fifty-years for Slazengers, the sporting goods company which has supplied Wimbledon with its balls, nets and canvas since 1902. He rose to be managing director and chairman before his retirement in 1976 and until 1983 was the company's non-executive chairman. 'Just because this is our club and tennis is our sport doesn't mean the members of the committee do not use their professional acumen,' he says. 'We are a committee but we are not any less able than if we were a board.'

Indeed, there cannot be many boards of commercial companies with a full-time staff of only sixty-four who have had the foresight to invest more than £20 million in capital improvements raised entirely from debenture stock while at the same time making 'profits' of about £23 million, as the Wimbledon committee have done during the last ten years.

Hadingham's own involvement, since his election to the chair in 1983 following the retirement of Air Chief Marshall Sir Brian Burnett, has bordered on full-time. He lives on Wimbledon Hill a few minutes' drive away, and he tends to be at the club most days. 'It's not all together unlike running Slazengers. The heads of department run the show and I wouldn't think to interfere but there are always decisions that only the chairman can take.'

He chairs eight full committee meetings in a year, sits in as an ex-officio member at the more important of the fifty-four sub-committee meetings and has a permanent presence during the Wimbledon fortnight. 'He is a working chairman, here in the offices most days, and we work closely together,' says Gorringe. The fact that the 'office' of the chairman – a man who, as

Gorringe admits, many believe still to be chairman of world tennis – is only a spare desk in Gorringe's own room is just a homely reminder that not everything has changed at Wimbledon.

For Hadingham it is a labour of love. He has been a member since 1957 – even though his father was a member, he was on the waiting list for membership for ten years – and has served on the committee of management since 1976. He carries an association even in his first given name, Reginald, which was chosen by his mother after Wimbledon's four-times champion Reginald Doherty who had once proposed to her. 'I've always thought that had she accepted him, it might have improved my forehand.' As it happened, he never used the name, becoming known even to his mother as Buzzer after his brother's vain attempts to call him 'brother'. 'My first school was in Wimbledon and I've lived in the place for sixty of my seventy-two years,' he says. 'This is my local tennis club.'

It has not been what most people would regard as a local club since it spent £140,000 constructing its present facilities in 1922, any more than the Marylebone Cricket Club at Lord's or the Royal and Ancient Golf Club at St Andrews are locals' clubs. Membership is limited to 375 ladies and gentlemen, and few of those live close enough to use it regularly. The wait to become a member is so long that the competitive days of most are past before they achieve it and the club offers temporary annual membership to about 100 more active players so that it can continue to put out respectable club teams.

Quite when the commercial success of its championships became the overriding concern of the club is not recorded, although as long ago as 1922 the All England Ground Company was created to issue debenture stock. Hadingham and Gorringe do not believe that there was ever a conscious decision taken by the club to become business-like, and certainly not one that was minuted. 'Knowing those who were here before, the club was always that,' says the chief executive, although Hadingham remembers that in his time as managing director at Slazenger's he had to suggest to the committee that, after more than sixty years as their ball, net and canvas supplier, it might be time to offer something more tenable for a commercial company than a one-year contract. 'It was the longest and probably the most important contract which the company had but it had always been something of a gentlemen's agreement,' he says.

Gorringe suggests that if there were particular turning points, the first was as long ago as 1968 with the introduction of prize money for players and the second in 1972 when the club first appointed a professional agency to market its championships as an occasion for corporate hospitality. 'A philosophy evolved as we changed to meet the changing times,' he says.

Indeed, the greatest changes happened during the second half of the 1970s under the chairmanship of Burnett, a shy man with a military man's habit of calling everybody by surnames, who was responsible for putting Hadingham forward for the committee in 1976 on his retirement from Slazengers. It was during his period of office that, first, the Baganal Harvey Organization was appointed as the club's commercial agents and a year later Mark McCormack's International Management Group (IMG) was entrusted with the sale of television rights outside of Europe. And it is television, indisputably, that has changed Wimbledon.

The commentators in their little green boxes around the Centre Court intruded for the first time in 1937 when a few hundred Londoners were privileged to see the 'new wonder' of television in its first-ever outside broadcast coverage of British sport – twenty-five minutes of a men's singles match. But in the last dozen years TV's presence and influence has been pervasive. The interests – and financial promises – of American television even persuaded the committee to move the gentlemen's singles final from a Saturday to a Sunday in 1982, and by 1987 the 'privileged few' who watched through the medium had become an audience of 350 million in eighty countries for the final alone. A survey done for the club of the 1985 coverage revealed that 837.02 hours of play were shown on a total of 440,821,005 television sets, reaching as far from Church Road as Venezuela, the Soviet Union, Equador and the 6,000 sets in Swaziland.

The power of the 'box' is apparent in the income and expenditure account. In 1973 the receipts from tickets produced the bulk of the club's annual income. Prices have risen regularly since, quadrupling the cost of a Centre Court ticket and multiplying ground admission prices by ten, and yet as a proportion of the

Club's income admissions have fallen dramatically to little more than twenty per cent.

Television fees, meanwhile, which were not a fifth of the income in the early seventies, have increased to more than sixty per cent of it, around £9 million in 1987. The US network NBC, cable's Home Box Office, Japan's NHK and Australia's Channel Nine all now produce their own live programmes, and together they pay considerably more than the BBC does for its ninety hours of coverage or, indeed, the European Broadcasting Union does for that whole continent.

As the fame and prestige of Wimbledon has been spread by television, so has the desire of companies to share in it. How they could be involved was the problem the committee, and its consultants at Baganal Harvey, had to deal with. They felt that sponsorship was inappropriate. The thought that each of the five competitions might have a commercial name attached to it horrified members. But then IMG came up with the alternative of licensing and marketing Wimbledon's own name, a device they employed successfully with the British Open on behalf of the Royal and Ancient Golf Club.

So in 1978 the symbol of a flying 'W' was created alongside the traditional crossed rackets logo of the championships, and IMG proposed Japan, where there was a high consumer demand for premium products marketed under prestigious names, as a trial market. Only the best, it was decided, would be good enough to bear Wimbledon's signature. 'Quality rather than volume,' says Gorringe, who was responsible for the project initially, in conjunction with IMG.

Soon there were ten licencees in Japan marketing products such as tennis clothing, shoes, and even wallets, belts, luggage and sunglasses. Kunnan Enterprises, the world's largest racket producers, now market a Wimbledon racket and 60,000 of the most expensive model were sold in the United States in 1986. 'Puts me in direct competition with Slazengers,' says Hadingham wryly, 'but what Wimbledon has done to popularize tennis world-wide has created a market big enough for everybody.' In fact, Slazengers themselves have taken the world-wide licence to market tennis balls under the Wimbledon name.

In 1985, a network of licencees was also established in the US, marketing a high quality range of tennis and leisure wear through the top department stores, with rackets, bags, hats and visors through sports shops. Non-sporting licences are now being taken up by British companies. Royal Doulton took a world-wide licence for English bone china and Wilkin and Sons for preserves. It is now possible to sleep in Wimbledon sheets or under their blankets, to dry on their towels, eat off their china, wear their clothing from head-to-toe and send letters on their stationery. You can even plan ahead on their calendars.

So successful had the project become that in April, 1985, the club appointed a former Slazenger marketing man, Rob McCowan, a man fluent in four languages, as its first marketing director. 'I just didn't have the expertise,' admits Gorringe. 'And it was important that we were not only represented by agents. The club had to be seen to be closely involved and not remote from licencees. They are part of our family and one of Rob's concerns is after-care and liaison with them.'

The club regard the marketing operation as insurance as much as income. 'For the first time we are not completely tied to the success of one fortnight each year,' says Gorringe. 'Our eggs aren't all in one basket and we are earning money the year round.'

The 1985 accounts, the last available which go into any detail, give a figure of £2 million for the proceeds of marketing and promotions, but a part of it comes from the lease of hospitality units during The Championships – those colourful marquees that dot the grounds during The Championships where companies wine and dine their guests.

The first hospitality unit, on one of Wimbledon's hard courts, was rented to an insurance company, Commercial Union, in 1975 when they were sponsoring the world-wide Grand Prix tournament circuit. Now there are forty-four, some taken exclusively by one company and others rented piece-meal. More than 100 companies are represented during the fortnight. The price is high. A table for eight for one day costs up to £2,000 but there is no shortage of companies wanting to take them.

Limitations have been imposed by the club itself, not only because of the pressure of space on its forty-two acres but also because of the pressure on its seating capacity on the Centre and Number One Courts. 'Each marquee holder is guaranteed sixteen

Centre and ten Number One tickets every day, and if we had to give more, we could only take them from the allocation to the public or to Britain's tennis clubs,' says Gorringe.

'Like Topsy, it just growed,' says Hadingham. 'I suppose we did become much more aggressive once we had agents like Baganal Harvey to tell us what things like catering contracts were worth. We hadn't been very market-orientated but we became conscious of what the market would take. We demanded more.'

Criticisms have been voiced that the commercial tail began to wag the old dog of a championship. Prices soared. A cartoon in Wimbledon's own programme for the 1987 championships showed a young lady eating strawberries who is saying to her escort: 'Sweet of you to sell your yacht and horses to buy me these.' Yet Town and County, who have the catering contract, still sold more than eighteen tons of strawberries, nine tons of salmon and smoked salmon and 12,000 bottles of champagne.

Wimbledon's audience is happy, it seems, to pay the prices if only they are offered entrance. The annual ballot for Centre and Number One Court tickets (up to £25 each for the finals) has been over-subscribed every year since 1924, and there have been murmurs for a number of years that too many have been withdrawn from the public ballot for sale to commercial companies. To be precise on any day it is 705 for the Centre Court and 440 for Number One Court which go to companies, which is little more than five per cent, but it is noticeable when many of these commercially important people do not take their seats, preferring to enjoy the hospitality within their marquees while watching the play on the closed circuit televisions. The social status of Wimbledon is such that those who wish to be able to say they have been are not usually those who go with a wish to watch the tennis.

A glance at public courts in Britain once Wimbledon is forgotten for another year is a reminder that Wimbledon's popularity is not tennis's. So has been the paltry attendance of spectators at Britain's own national closed championships at Telford.

Yet for all the British public's apparent indifference to the game most of the year — and the inability of generations of the nation's players to succeed at it in an international context — the All-England Club has been unable from the earliest days to cope with the popularity of its championships. In 1880, before the club owned its own ground or had any permanent stands, there were more than a thousand spectators, and on Friday, July 4 1913, there was the first crowd of 10,000. Wimbledon's library records the first evidence of touts that day with tickets changing hands at £7 10s (£7.50). By 1932, 200,000 spectators were attending during the two weeks of the championships and when, at the one hundredth championship in 1986, the aggregate rose above 400,000 and almost 40,000 crowded the grounds on a single day, the committee was forced to call a halt to the growth. 'We like people to leave having enjoyed their tennis, not complaining that they haven't seen anything,' says Gorringe.

The following year the gates were closed whenever 28,000 were inside, although, in the event, it reduced the attendance during the fortnight by only 4,000. 'We are bursting at the seams,' says Hadingham. 'We have sufficient courts but not enough room for spectators or for all the companies who would like to do business with us.'

There is nowhere for the club to expand. There are roads on all sides, and a public golf course and houses beyond them. The local council have accepted an application to build three further covered courts on the other side of Somerset Road which will take land from a car park used only for two weeks each year. Meanwhile, enterprising local residents take advantage of the over-crowding by leasing their gardens to companies for the entertaining of their clients.

Another possibility is the building of more spectator accommodation on the existing courts. 'It may come to that,' says Hadingham. But if 128 players are to continue to go into the draw for the gentlemen's singles there would need to be more playing time. That would mean breaking with the tradition of starting play on Centre and Number One Courts at two in the afternoon which the committee did a few years ago for the outside courts, starting play there at 12.30pm.

The most pragmatic committee member might think long and hard before upsetting the tradition of the Royal Box party of arriving at ten minutes to two, particularly when the club president is the Duke of Kent, a tennis enthusiast. Hadingham once chose not to tell him of a bomb threat which had been telephoned to the offices because it might disturb his enjoyment. 'We had decided it was a hoax,' he explained.

The alternative is to stop growing, to limit attendances, stop selling hospitality units and, as Hadingham sees it, 'devote ourselves to keeping Wimbledon as number one in the world'. But there is another unspoken pressure. The Championships have not been an end in themselves for a long time but the only successful means which British tennis has found of making the money it believes can produce the domestic players who could get results at Wimbledon and in turn popularize the playing of the game.

Since 1934, the ownership of the land and buildings at Wimbledon has been vested in the All England Ground Company, a company jointly owned with the Lawn Tennis Association, the national governing body of the sport. The agreement gives the club the right to stage the major national championships but in return it has to turn over to the LTA the money remaining after payment of the club's and The Championships' expenses, 'for the furtherance of the game'. It is an agreement which runs until 1999 and which allows the LTA to nominate seven of their own council to sit with Wimbledon's twelve committee members on all matters relating to the championships; the club retaining not only a majority but also the chair.

It is a unique relationship between a private club and a national body which has had a chequered past, both before and since the agreement formally brought them together. At present, Wimbledon describe it is as better than ever and it may help that the LTA's executive director, Ian Peacock, used to work for Hadingham at Slazenger. That the LTA are so beholden may also have something to do with it. They could afford to be less than grateful when Wimbledon was a £50,000 benefactor but who would dare spit in the face of a million-pound fairy godmother?

'When it was £50,000 we didn't much worry what happened to it,' says Hadingham. 'Now it would be irresponsible of us to hand over £7 million and not be interested.' So twice yearly they meet the LTA management committee, to hear their plans and influence them. 'Our money cannot buy the qualities you need to be a Wimbledon champion: the heart, the physique, the determination, the talent; but I would expect the sort of sums we're giving to produce a quarter-finalist or two, even a semi-finalist.'

The governing body of British tennis has become dependent totally on the All England Club's championships. In 1986, their accounts showed their income as £6,800,000, of which only £350,000 came from sources other than Wimbledon's 1985 surplus or from the interest on the investment of previous surpluses. It was a sum so vast that the LTA spent only £3,700,000 of it on tennis during the year, had to give away £1,700,000 in tax and put in reserve £1,750,000. Curiously, it has even been able, over recent years to lend, interest-free, £2,400,000 of Wimbledon's money to the Queen's Club, another exclusive private club in London in which the LTA holds a 95.6 per cent stake.

Yet Gorringe, who is one of two Wimbledon representatives on the LTA council, admits that there is a desire from that quarter for more money. 'It's never a demand or even a request and they appreciate that we are not a bottomless pit but you sense, how shall I say, a hope. They are trying to generate income of their own but for the foreseeable future we will continue to provide between eighty and ninety per cent of their income. Our relationship will work so long as we continue to maintain standards and are not forced always to look for the last buck.'

The LTA may have to make do with less in future. The club committee are contemplating siphoning something off from the surplus in case of a 'rainy day' and it might be thought imprudent of them to be as unprotected as at present. Their spending from the income is closely controlled and audited for the LTA, and nobody has suggested that the committee are anything but good caretakers of tennis' national seedcorn. 'We are not a charity in either sense of the word,' says Gorringe.

There is also the pressure on Wimbledon to ensure that players fresh from the shale courts of the French Open in Paris have competitive opportunities to readjust to grass before Wimbledon, and already the club give £300,000 to help other British tournaments in the two weeks before the championships.

Fortunately for the LTA, the club does not covet the money it makes. Hadingham's motivation – apart, he says, from maintaining Wimbledon's status – is to see as much money as possible raised for the game in Britain. 'What else would we do with all that money anyway?' he asks. 'Set up our own LTA? We're not interested in the role. Whatever we say to the LTA – and we're pretty close to them – is never critical but constructive.'

The club committee is so parsimonious in handling what becomes of the LTA's money that very few pounds of the vast sum it has spent on general improvements to the club in the last ten years have come from money which would have gone to the LTA. Almost entirely, capital expenditure has derived from the same non-tennis source that built the national home of tennis in the first place sixty-five years ago – the purchasers of its debenture stock.

The 2,100 £500 debentures were issued in 1922 to finance the purchase of the ground and the buildings on it. Each can be renewed at a premium every five years, the present holders invariably taking up their option which on the last occasion in 1986 cost £5,000, raising £10,050,000 for the club. The actual £500 is returnable should the holder not wish to renew.

For their £5,000 debenture, holders get a free Centre Court ticket for each day of each championship during the five years. They are entitled to access to the debenture holders' lounge and an opportunity to purchase a car parking season ticket. But it is the Centre Court ticket which makes the debentures so valuable. One debenture traded on the Stock Market before the 1987 championships for £22,500 with only four championships remaining of its value. After that championship, the value with three remaining was still close to £20,000, but it is precisely because so few are traded – and because Wimbledon tickets are so precious – that the price is high.

Since 1976 the debenture holders have paid for Wimbledon to build four more courts, to raise the roof of the Centre Court to give room for 1,000 more seats, to build two new stands for Number One Court, extend those at Numbers Two, Three and the East Stand of Centre Court and, appropriately, build a lounge for debenture holders. They have also financed the construction of a new, members' enclosure and the rebuilding of the lady-members' changing rooms.

Those last two improvements are not insignificant. It is too easily forgotten that the All England Club remains a club with members who use it, and Hadingham admits to being 'very conscious' of the danger of putting business first. In 1983 members did become concerned that Gorringe and his staff were too busy running a business to administer the club, and a new paid club secretary, Roger Ambrose, was appointed to take over in that department, organizing the social side, the club's internal competitions and inter-club games.

There is a waiting list for membership of 830 going back to people first proposed in the 1920s and never likely now to be admitted. There were only six new members elected in 1987, replacing six who died. But what they are offered beyond the status and the automatic right to Wimbledon tickets might not be thought satisfactory in many clubs. 'It's not all that tremendous being a member, which is why we only ask £30 subscription,' says Hadingham.

The disadvantages are not obvious seeing the tasteful, light, panelled members' drawing room and bar, the dining room and the sporting facilities but, as Gorringe says, 'it's not a bed of roses for a member'. The use of grass courts is severely restricted because of the demands of the championships and the time the club's ten permanent groundsmen need to prepare them, and from May to the middle of July the hard courts have marquees on them. They can have their say at the annual meeting, and it is the members who elect the twelve among them who serve on the committee, but most problems are sorted out quietly with a friendly word. 'We would not want to take the members for granted,' says Gorringe, 'but more of them are seen here during the fortnight than at any other time. For them, as much as the public, it is the highlight and they accept that sacrifices have to be made for it.'

There are limits. Clearly Wimbledon could make far better use of the facilities, and it must be tempting to make an arena, with a spectator capacity of 14,500 in a highly-populated part of south-west London used for only two weeks in a year, more cost efficient. Hadingham, however, is a realist. He won a Military Cross and bar commanding 302 Battery of the Anti-Tank Regiment against German Panzers in Salerno in 1943 but he is not willing to confront members and local residents. 'They suffer enough with one annual upheaval when they cannot get their cars from their drives and need an army to clear litter from their lawns,' he says.

There are also the club's own lawns to be considered. Wimbledon is synonymous with lawn tennis. 'Grass is written in our tablets,' says Gorringe, 'and having it limits what else we can do.' The committee have discovered that it is physically possible to put another structure over the grass on the Centre Court without touching it but nobody is willing to take the chance.

But the most precious property a chairman of the All England Club and his management committee must protect is the image. 'There is a mystique about Wimbledon which might be tarnished if we did things like pop concerts or big fights,' says Gorringe. 'To most people, Wimbledon is tennis.'

It is this great trust invested in the officials that weighs on every decision. Hadingham, as the club chairman, accepts that he is perceived by the public to be chairman of the game. In reality, he is not entitled by the position to sit on the International Tennis Federation management committee, or the men's and women's professional councils or even the LTA council. But when the public want to let off steam about tennis it is to Wimbledon they write and Hadingham who replies. 'Most of the flak about McEnroe's behaviour came my way,' he says.

Wimbledon underpins the game's traditions throughout the world and what it does has a bearing on all, as the world discovered in 1968 when a unilateral decision of the club and LTA to admit professionals to The Championships forced the ITF to abolish the distinction between amateurs and professionals everywhere. Its chairman's clout in the corridors of power is considerable, and so is the responsibility on him to protect the institution for the future.

Hadingham reckons that he could make another £5 million every year just by putting advertising in the arena or calling the gentlemen's and ladies' singles by a sponsor's name. He has been approached by several companies who would be interested. It would be an easy way to make money, not involving effort or organization. 'But it won't happen as long as I'm chairman. Nor will we have a different surface to grass. On those two issues, I'm inflexible.'

What's right for Wimbledon is Hadingham's yardstick. There is a growing pressure from players to move The Championships back one week to give them more time to adjust to a grass surface, and he is listening. 'If they could persuade Ascot, Henley, the British Open and the Test matches to move as well to accommodate BBC's schedule, we might go along. For us it is always a question of quality, tradition and the ambience of the place. The club's changed hugely since I became a member in how it looks, in the buildings. In other ways, it has changed very little, and that's how we want to keep it.

'None of us at the club are doing it for the money. Every year, on the day before The Championships when I address the men players at a meeting, I tell them that. If I thought that I was just doing it to make them richer I would jack it in tomorrow.'

But richer he is making them. In 1968 when the Australian Rod Laver won his third singles title at the first 'Open' Wimbledon, his prize was £2,000. In 1987 he would have earned £80 more losing in the first round, and semi-finalist would have earned almost £10,000 more than the entire prize fund of that first year. Pat Cash, the gentlemen's singles winner, earned himself £155,000.

Hadingham thinks Wimbledon pays too much now – it rose by more than sixteen per cent in 1987 – but it is his choice. The four Grand Slam tournaments: Wimbledon, the French, US and Australian Opens, decide their own prize funds independently, and at Wimbledon it is Hadingham and Gorringe who make the recommendations. 'We pay too much but we have to be comparable, and in 1987 the US Open paid both its singles champions a quarter of a million dollars. I find that staggering for seven matches but it's the name of the game. The players contribute to our financial success and it's only right that they should receive a fair reward for that contribution.'

Hadingham is proud of his relationship with the players. Burnett, a serviceman, was not strong on public relations, but players acknowledge that Hadingham has changed the atmosphere. His letter to McEnroe before one championships when the champion's behaviour was creating headlines was a masterpiece of diplomacy, and he makes a point of meeting the players before The Championships and during them with Ted Tinling, whom the committee have appointed as the liaison man with the players. 'The club used to be weak on aspects of the modern game but since first Mark Cox and then John Feaver and Virginia Wade were appointed to the committee we have been better able to appreciate their needs,' he says. Typical was the decision in 1987 to give all players £50 each day they remain in the championships to help defray the costs of their accommodation, a constant source of complaint previously because of the price of London hotels during high summer. Hadingham's rewards have been what he calls 'happy' championships in 1986 and 1987.

Wimbledon's growth, he thinks, must slow eventually. Maintaining the quality will put a brake on the expansion of volume. The prize money will rise less quickly ('just a bit of fine tuning to shake any anomalies') and so will the surplus. The increases were more than one-third for each of three years, then twenty-six per cent in 1985, fifteen per cent in 1986 and 'we mustn't expect records every year,' says Hadingham. His greater concern is that during his chairmanship Wimbledon continues to be 'number one in the world'. And as he says: 'I don't think you look at the surplus to decide that.'

3
THE COMPETITOR

IN THE conference room of the Europa in Stuttgart, a commercial hotel in the city's industrial quarter, Sebastian Coe is going about his business. There is a gold medal to be won the following day at the European Athletics Championships but for the moment there is a living to be made. Today he is promoting the sale of shoes.

Before him are media men; some Italian, a few German, many British, all seeking a story, some hoping for a private interview, others hanging around on the chance of a gift of a pair of shoes. Most of the faces and many of the names are known to him, and the occasion is relaxed, the questioning is about himself rather than the shoes.

Coe wears anonymous blue jeans and anonymous sweater but sticking out from under the top table on the fastest feet in the room are The Product, shoes by Diadora Inc. of Milan, the hosts of the gathering. This is the soft sell, promotion by association. The company's executives stay in the background. There is time later for the hard talking when Coe meets the company's major retailers.

Coe is an easy man for them to work with. 'A real pro,' says one Italian. Appearances like this are only part of his work for them. He is a consultant, advising on shoe design and testing prototypes; a model for their advertising campaigns and, critically, he is an international shop window when he runs, the Diadora logo on his shoes obvious to all.

He is the only international star in Diadora's stable of athletes. The others are Italians, champions of Europe, such as Stefano Mei, the 5,000 metres champion, but not international names like Coe. He is a three-letter household word, an answer in *Trivial Pursuits* no less, and a sporting name which, like Pele, Borg and Ali, transcends the boundaries of the sporting world. The Olympic Games often equates to excellence in the public mind and Coe's two Olympic victories in the Blue Riband event of 1,500 metres ensure not only his sporting immortality but also his value in the market place. What he wears on his feet when he runs is worth £100,000 to him of any company's money.

He has endorsed and advertised the shoes of Diadora and the clothing of C & A, and before them the shoes and clothing of the US company Nike. At another time he promoted the usefulness of ICI's clothing fibre Tactel by wearing sportswear made from it, and he is a consultant to Blue Arrow, an international employment agency, paid substantially for fifteen days' work over three years.

Yet ten years ago, when Coe was a relative newcomer to the British athletics team, the endorsement of any product would have guaranteed athletic oblivion, a life ban for the heinous crime of earning money by capitalizing on fame gained from the sport. Under the rules of the International Amateur Athletic Federation merely to coach another runner for payment was punishable then by life banishment from all athletic competition.

The athletes known to the world for their Olympic achievements were amateurs. From the Latin, *amo*, to love. They were, as the Oxford English Dictionary put it, 'ones who cultivate things as a pastime'.

It was a concept of class divisions, created by Victorians to keep people in their rightful places. The sport of cricket went so far as to call their annual match between professionals and amateurs, 'Gentlemen versus Players'. The forerunner of today's Amateur Athletic Association, the Amateur Athletic Club, in 1867 had in its rules a definition of an amateur which read: 'An amateur is any person who has never competed in open competition or for public money and who has never at any period in his life taught or assisted in the pursuit of athletic exercises as a means of livelihood or as a mechanic, artisan or labourer.'

The Club allowed what it called 'lower classes' to compete in its championships but not to become members. In 1892 a professional who masqueraded as an amateur in a race was sent to prison 'with hard labour' for one month. In 1896 five athletes, including two world record holders who received £5 for 'attending' a race, today's appearance fee, were banned for life. It was another year before athletes were allowed even to have the costs of travelling to competitions reimbursed by their organizers.

The motives of the Victorian establishment were not the affectations of class but they were hardly honourable. The gentleman amateur, well-bred and well-heeled, scorned effort. Natural gifts were what mattered, and to attempt to improve on them by training was a vulgarity. Only the working classes did that and, to keep competition among the better classes fair, they had to be excluded. Money was not at the root of their fear; it was a way of separating those to be blackballed, the working men for whom physical effort had meaning only if it was rewarded.

Eventually and ironically, those who would defend the legacy of the Victorians were the Marxist-Leninists of the Socialist bloc who found the system suited them as it had the English establishment, and for the same reason. It kept out those in the West who would be able to afford to train full-time, as the Socialist nations' own state-funded 'amateur' competitors could. It reduced the competition.

So, far into the twentieth century, athletes of all sports were restricted and exploited by a sporting establishment seeking to perpetuate a system conceived with ignoble intentions. The hypocrisies practised were often absurd, and the anomalies indefensible. Athletes, told to wear the names of a meeting's sponsor on the back and front of their running vests like sandwich boards, would be damned if they advertised the same product for their own benefit. A long distance runner could be banned because he boxed for a fee in a fairground booth, as John Tarrent was for receiving £75 in the sixties. Olympic high jump bronze medallist Dwight Stones was excluded for a time because he had participated for a money prize in a television programme called *Superstars* which bore no relationship to high jumping.

Coe himself almost fell foul of the rules in 1978 before he was well known. He ran in a meeting in Gateshead sponsored by the Dutch electrical company Philips. He and his father travelled from Sheffield, and received a total of £200 in expenses. It was hardly excessive and far less than other, better-known athletes received at the same meeting, but it was more than could be reasonably justified for the trip. It was common practice as the governing bodies of Western countries usually turned a blind eye, but on this occasion the meeting was organized by a local council governed more strictly by statutory provisions. Two local opposition councillors objected and demanded to see the books – a mass of undetailed claims and unsigned receipts. More than £9,000 had been paid out but there were few signatures. One who had signed for his money claimed to be Mickey Mouse.

The case became a cause célèbre, and led directly to Britain becoming a leading proponent of moves to rid the sport of the existing amateur rules. But, at the time, the Amateur Athletic Association was forced to investigate. Only the intervention of Derek Cole, a club official and private school headmaster who had legal training, who tied the investigation up with threats of legal proceedings, saved the athletes from more detailed examinations.

Even then, unknown to the athletic authorities, Coe and his father were guarding themselves against the legal ramifications of the illegal system by the creation of a company in their home city of Sheffield. All Coe's 'excessive expenses' went into the company, which had an independent director of impeccable pedigree, and all profits were declared to the Inland Revenue. 'In fact its sole purpose was to declare income to the Revenue at a time when it was not legal within the sport for an athlete to have any,' says Coe. 'Our attitude was that the main concern was not the sport because at worst I could only fall foul of rules unlikely to be upheld by the courts. We were concerned with playing it straight within the laws of the country and we kept the Revenue totally informed; and they knew what I was earning, whatever the rules of the sport at the time.'

It was the same for competitors in other sports afflicted by the curse of amateurism. The International Tennis Federation, the Marylebone Cricket Club and the Royal and Ancient Golf Club, in their own different ways and different spheres of influence, all

Sebastian Coe appearing in his first commercial for the Beecham food drink, the first occasion any athlete still active had been allowed to advertise on British television.

It pays to advertise – Boris Becker cashes in on his fame as a tennis player.

"Coca-Cola and Coke are registered trademarks which identify the same product of The Coca-Cola Company".

supported amateurism for long periods of this century. The controlling body of Rugby Union still thinks that way but among the major spectator sports of the world it is now a rarity.

All mention of the word 'amateur' has been struck from the rules of athletics, soccer and cricket. Tennis, which once refused to permit professionals to play on the same courts as amateurs, recognizes only 'players'. The West German weekly magazine *Stern* put Boris Becker's 1986 earnings at more than $10 million. The Italian clothing company Ellesse offered him $20 million to endorse their products for six years but lost to a reputed $27.5 million offer from Puma.

The playing of the game is almost incidental to Becker's earnings, little more than a tenth of it being won on the court. Playing promotes him as a product but beyond a certain point it becomes irrelevant. The British boxer Henry Cooper has continued to earn a sizeable income twenty years after his retirement, and Bjorn Borg earned more annually four years after his retirement than when he was Wimbledon champion.

Indeed many of the products the personalities of sport now endorse and advertise have no connection with sport. Jimmy Connors, the former Wimbledon champion, advertises the brokers Paine Webber. His rival Ivan Lendl promotes the Avis hire car chain. Becker is a client of Coca-Cola, Philips and Deutsche Bank.

Their effects on the companies they promote are often measurable. In 1984, the year before Becker signed a contract with Puma, a West German sports equipment manufacturer, the company sold 15,000 tennis rackets; the next year it sold 70,000 and in 1986 300,000. The company believes that Becker's Wimbledon victories generated sales of $50 million.

Ellesse, an up-market Italian clothing company, reckon that their sales increased by $3 million in West Germany alone when Becker won Wimbledon. His commission for the sales his name promoted was $450,000, and when he left them, accepting a single racket–clothing deal with Puma, Ellesse sales in West Germany fell by a fifth, exactly the amount they had risen when Becker endorsed them.

Becker is so important to Puma that they were easily persuaded to launch a range of rackets and shoes under the name of Ion

Tiriac, his 49-year-old manager, which retail at $360, labelled 'A Touch of Class'.

Lendl, the number one ranked tennis player, is seeded second to Becker in the world-wide commercial stakes, but the numbers are still huge. Adidas claim to sell more than $20 million a year of Lendl-endorsed products. The magazine *Sport*, in its annual survey of sporting earnings, calculated that Lendl's earnings off the court in 1986 were $6 million. One company, Ray-Ban, were paying him a fee every time he was pictured wearing their sunglasses. He was collecting royalties on sales of Bow Brand racket strings, a fee of $300,000 for wearing a tiny flash on one shoulder of his tennis shirts promoting the Gleneagles Country Club, and smaller fees for endorsing bread, calendars, an energy drink, a travel agency, a health programme and even golf clubs.

In 1987, in the USA, it was calculated that companies spent $500 million on using sportsmen and women to endorse, promote and advertise their products. The possibilities on offer in Britain were hinted at by a former agent of motor-racing driver Nigel Mansell, who sued him for £1.2 million over an alleged breach of a management contract.

Motor racing drivers have the right image for the type of product aimed at the young, upwardly mobile person, and it helps that they are inordinately well paid for what they do. Mansell, whose contract with the Williams team earns him more than $2 million a year, is paid more than $100,000 to promote the name of the West German fashion house of Hugo Boss on his driver's overalls, and another £250,000 as one of a team of sportsmen who represent the blue-chip chemical company ICI; not bad for a man who had to sell his semi-detached house to finance his early career as a driver in Formula 3.

Skiers are in the same division in the body-as-a-billboard league. They don't waste a moment at the finish of a race removing their skis to stand with them, manufacturer's name to the fore, to catch every second of television air-time. The 1986–7 World Cup champion Pirmin Zurbriggen's personal sponsor is the Swiss Bank Corporation and his Luxembourg rival Marc Girardelli is head-to-toe in the livery of Marlboro Leisure Wear, the subsidiary that promotes the colours and logo of the cigarette company.

Even sports commentators, those impartial observers of the games people play, have got in the act. John Madden, the former coach to the Oakland Raiders in the USA who became a sports-caster with CBS has been used to sell everything from spray paint to an investment firm. During 1987 he appeared in advertising for the Ramada Inn chain, Exxon motor oil, Miller Lite, McDonald's and Canon. His estimated income from commercial exploitation was $1 million and one deal with Greyhound bus lines gave him his own customized $500,000 bus with driver on twenty-four-hour call.

But business for Sebastian Coe grew out of forty-one days in 1979 in which he broke three world records: the 800 metres and mile in Oslo and the 1,500 metres in Zurich. It was a feat unprecedented in modern times and his life was transformed. Suddenly, letters arrived at his Sheffield home addressed only 'Sebastian Coe, Great Britain'. He was famous.

'Until then, sport had cost me money, or to be more accurate it had cost my parents money,' says Coe. 'I had this company to declare tax to the Revenue but I wasn't making money as such. It was always peanuts and it didn't cover the cost of petrol, the hotels you have to stay in as a young athlete, all my kit and shoes. I was sponsored, if you like, by my mother and father. That for me is the dominating theme of sport, that whatever sports people achieve in the end is due to long years of preparations when others have had to put their hands in their pockets. Look at British athletics. People ask what is the great thing about it, what's its system. There is none, just a lot of things contributing their bit, but the dominating theme to me is the family.

'When I won at the Olympics in Moscow (in 1980), I had my father to thank. Daley (Thompson) had his Auntie Doreen and Steve (Ovett) had his mother. All were dependent on them for most of their athletic careers, from when they started until they were big names earning money which made them independent. And that's a long time. I was running eleven years before I broke world records. Just think how much of my folk's petrol I'd used in that time.'

Becker's career became a business when his coach Gunther Bosch offered his professional management to Tiriac, a Romanian who controls a New York management group, T-V Enterprises. Lendl broke through commercially when he severed his connections with the Czech Tennis Federation and was actively sold in the market place by the Washington company ProServ Inc. But for Coe, business just evolved slowly as a consequence of continuing success on the track.

'Evolved would be the word,' he says. 'I don't think my career ever became a business in most people's understanding of the word. Even now in the genuine sense of business it isn't. There are components of it that are like a business, such as contracts and funds and tax management, and there is the management of time which is similar to business. But there was never a moment when my father or I thought that we could make money at this and we should put down a three-year plan or anything to exploit it. It just happened without us doing much at all.'

In the summer of 1979 when he was setting the first of eight world records which were to fall to him, he was also occupied with his final examinations as a student of economics at Loughborough University. His father, Peter, was a production director of a cutlery manufacturer in the steel city of Sheffield. To have the business-side of a professional sportsman suddenly thrust upon them, as well, was a burden neither wanted.

'At first it was just answering thousands of letters, and handling the demands of the media, the constant phone calls, the would-be sponsors. That was hard. My whole family was affected and involved. But by 1980 it had become an intolerable strain. My old man had three factories to run, a family and my training, and the other business was the limit.'

In the autumn of 1980, father and son sat down to find a solution. 'He is a trained industrial manager. It was not beyond his ability to handle contracts but while he was happy to do it, it was pretty obvious that his greatest value to me as an athlete was coaching me to become a faster runner. It was pretty obvious that we needed outside help, if only to take away some of the pressure and allow us to go on athletically without constantly cutting short training sessions to discuss business with somebody.'

The answer was to ask the International Management Group to handle business matters for him; a decision which, seven years later, hardly seems dramatic but which, at the time, commanded headlines in newspapers. Athletes were amateurs still, or at least supposed to be. They did not have agents. Coe, indeed, was the first British athlete to appoint one.

'People who have not experienced it cannot appreciate how debilitating the commercial pressures are. Everybody wants a piece of you when all you are concerned with at the time is achieving your goals in sport. Really, it's not promotion you need but protection. You can't turn your back on money. There is no way an athlete of my calibre or Daley's or Cram's should as long as it is not injurious to themselves or the sport. But at the same time, if you are going to succeed, you must keep it at arm's length. You can't be devoured by it. Too many successful people in sport allow that to happen. They forget that sport is what it's about first of all.'

When Coe first ran, sport was all it was about. 'I was brought up to believe that all that mattered in the end was the Olympic Games. That was the pinnacle everybody set before you. You ran to prove yourself at every level and in the hope that one day you would reach the ultimate level. Money didn't enter your head, certainly not if you were lucky enough, as I was, to have parents who could afford to pay your way.'

Indeed, money ceased to be a concern for the three years before the 1980 Olympic Games because Coe was receiving financial grants from the Sports Aid Foundation, an organization independent of sport's governing bodies but which works closely with them to raise money to assist *amateur* competitors with grants based on their financial needs.

'When I went to IMG with my father in late 1980 it was not because I needed money or to make more money. It was because the commercial pressure was threatening to get in the way of what mattered; which was my running. It was important that I went on running, and running successfully, if I was to make the most of the commercial possibilities over a long period. It was also clear that I should get on with what I was best at and leave other areas to those better at them.'

There were no people with more experience of looking after the sporting élite than IMG, a business with annual revenues exceeding £300 million, offices in fifteen cities including London and clients as fabulously wealthy as Chris Evert, Martina Navratilova and Bjorn Borg. They could do everything for a

client, from managing tax and investments to negotiating perfor-
mance fees – leaving the client only to play the game. What they
had little experience of was working with competitors from a
sport controlled by a set of rules whose purpose was to prevent
them doing almost anything which came naturally to IMG. Like
making a profit.

Initially, for appearance's sake and as a gesture towards the
rules which still forbade money and agents, Peter Coe was
announced as IMG's client. 'In fact, I never did have a contract
with them,' says Seb. But the arrangement was that they handled
everything for the runner, even to the extent of acting for him in
negotiations with race organizers and as a shield for him in his
relations with the media. 'They took on everything and, to be
fair, they had their strengths,' he says. But in that opinion there is
an unspoken qualification.

IMG had grown up in golf where professionalism had been
accepted for generations. They had been the catalyst for enormous financial growth for players of the game, and eventually
also for tennis players when that sport went 'open' and prospered.
Athletics was not their domain.

Coe realized it within months. The executives appointed to
handle his affairs would have marketing expertise but Coe himself would have to educate them in the ways of the sport, its
nuances and politics. A sport in which the bottom line was not
profit and which had existed for 100 years without concern for it
was foreign to them. 'It was horrifically difficult for them because
of the nature of the sport,' says Coe. 'With somebody like Nigel
Mansell, his sport has been commercially established for forty or
fifty years. There are ground rules established, traditions, and
everybody knows where they stand. Ours wasn't. It was a culture
shock for athletics officials to have to sit down with people called
agents. They were used to dealing direct with athletes. If a
meeting organizer wanted me to run, he would call me, or my
father. Even now, almost ten years into a commercial sport, they
are loathe to talk to agents.'

So Coe began to limit his involvement with IMG. 'From the
start I had kept back some commercial links already established.
Then I realized that I had my own well-established links with the
media, people I'd grown up with in the sport over the previous six

years or so, and it was strange for them suddenly to have to reach me via an agent. I didn't want people asking fees of these people. And then there were the things I'd always been willing to do for nothing, like children's television.'

IMG handled other commercial arrangements, their forte, but within strictly-controlled parameters laid down by Coe. There was to be nothing of what, he called 'tacky'. The work was to be with clean, wholesome products for acceptable companies. The image was all important, both his own and his sport's, but it was more than that. Coe was thinking long-term from his earliest involvement with business, to what he calls the 'after-life' when he is no longer on the nation's television screens as a runner.

Almost immediately he turned down a three-year contract for television commercials with the deodorant company Fabergé for their men's range of Brut. Boxer Henry Cooper and world champion motorcycle rider Barry Sheene had both 'splashed on' the Brut products on the TV but somehow Coe could not see himself as right in the part. 'Perhaps I was being ultra-careful but people should remember that who you take from today, you take from for ever. You set your niche in the market and stay there. You can't sell to different groups and retain your market credibility.'

IMG were keen to accept Brut. They tried to persuade him. Coe was adamant in his opposition. 'I had this instinctive feeling that it wasn't right for me. It wasn't about image, or what I thought my image was but about how I felt. And I didn't feel comfortable with a deodorant ad. I felt that there is a public perception of you and it's difficult to break once established. I was looking long-term, I suppose, knowing that you can't do a down-market commercial one month and go up market the next.'

A few weeks later he accepted an offer to do a twenty-second television commercial for the pharmaceutical company Beecham's hot drink Horlicks, the first television commercial to be done by a British athlete who was still competing. 'It was pitched at the right public in my opinion. I felt comfortable with it.'

Coe has put strict limits on the work he does, not by turning it away but by setting his standards so high that there are few takers. He will not open shops or make after-dinner speeches, and he is not interested in one-off jobs for companies. He did only one in 1987, making a speech for Barclays International, at a management conference in Portugal. Another speaker there was Giscard d'Eistang, former President of France. 'That was the sort of level I consider right, and, at that level, it is inevitable that there are not many possibilities. On the other hand, I've put myself in a market where few sports people go or would want to go. From the beginning I worked on the theory that while I was not going to make as much as by opening super-markets every other day or making after-dinner jokes, it might put me in an area which I could sustain for ten or twenty years beyond my career.' It is no coincidence, then, that the first fee he ever received off the track was for a speech he gave to the senior management of Hambro, nor that he used the opportunity to draw for them the parallels between sporting and business success.

In Rome in September 1981, at a special congress of the International Amateur Athletic Federation the rule on the eligibility of athletes, once known as the amateur rule, had been changed to allow athletes to endorse and advertise. Even so, the contract had to be between the advertiser and the athlete's national federation, and payment for it had to be made to the federation who, 'after deducting any percentage considered appropriate, can pay the remaining part to an athletic fund'.

These funds were the sport's way of continuing the pretence that, at the top end, it was a recreation still, a pastime. What an athlete earned was to be paid into the funds administered by trustees representing the national federation and the athlete. The athlete was allowed to draw expenses from the fund but could not take it all until retirement from the sport. It was a call, as the Yale professor Bob Giegengack once said of a similar International Olympic Committee proposal, to 'let's all be a little bit pregnant'.

The advantage to the sport was obvious. Their national federations maintained control, something that always had a crucial bearing on their thinking. Theoretically, all contracts and earnings went through them, and they held the purse strings, even taking a percentage (a sliding scale to a maximum of fifteen per cent in Britain) for their efforts. But in practice what was allowed as an expense was so comprehensive that athletes could live on what they earned, setting mortgages, car hire purchase and food against the fund.

It was an arrangement as phoney as the under-the-counter payments for wearing a manufacturer's shoes or running a certain race which the athletic authority had been turning a blind eye to for years. 'In theory the commission which the British Athletic Board took from my contract with Horlicks was to help the grass roots of the sport; in reality it was a payment for a waiver allowing me to by-pass their constitution's rules on amateur status. It was a straight commercial deal – we waive the rules if you pay us the money. And very quickly you were talking in terms of big money. The cut they took from people like myself, Cram, Thompson and Ovett around 1983 and 1984 was saving them from a major cash-flow crisis.'

But the most contentious area of the relationship between him, his sport, his agents and his livelihood, for that's what it had become, was his competitive programme. IMG were accustomed to handling the competitive schedules of golfers and tennis players. It was natural for them to assume responsibility for Coe's programme, for negotiations and arrangements, at least in the international invitation meetings which were not directly under the control of governing bodies.

Coe was a valuable property. He had the most famous name in world athletics and, more pertinently, a name always connected with that of another superlative British athlete, Steve Ovett, a runner of the same events who was only eleven months older but had been established internationally four years before Coe. Ovett was the 1977 World Cup and 1978 European 1,500 metres champion. He had beaten Coe in the Olympic 800 metres, and lost to him in the Olympic 1,500 metres. Coe had set a world mile record in 1979 which Ovett had improved in 1980; Coe had regained it in 1981 and Ovett had broken it again.

There was rivalry enough, but the media were happy to improve on it. Ovett, enigmatic and unapproachable, was labelled the bad guy; Coe, open and friendly, was the good guy. And the two had not met in a race outside a major championship since their early teens. For an agent, it was a custom-made best seller, and IMG set out to hawk it to the highest bidder.

In the autumn of 1981 they succeeded; the best of three races between the two over different distances the following summer in the United States, Britain and on the continent. It would be the most lucrative foot race in history, worth more than £100,000 each to Coe and Ovett.

It never happened because Ovett ran into church railings while on a training run and was never properly fit during 1982. And Coe himself was unwell with a virus infection by August. But the furore the event created, the undue importance attached to it when to both athletes the European Championships that year were more significant, persuaded Coe that his competitive programme should revert to the control of his father and himself. 'We decided that we couldn't maintain control of the build-up to championships if somebody else was involved in arranging parts of the racing programme.'

Coe believes now that the projected series with Ovett was a miscalculation and the fact that it did not happen could even have been pivotal to the sport's evolution, just as Jack Nicklaus' refusal to play exhibition matches against Johnny Miller in preference to tournament play was to golf. 'I'm glad it didn't happen,' says Coe. 'We could have ended up taking the sport down the wrong road. To be honest, IMG singularly failed to appreciate the nature of athletics and in part perhaps that was my fault. All their other clients were in tennis or golf, or professional sports. They could not understand that there were things you could not buy. Perhaps that's the American mentality. But European track and field could not be approached that way. You could not take a cheque book to them and buy them. They had been around too long, doing it their way and doing it pretty well.

'I spent many hours discussing it with IMG's people but they never comprehended. Even after another five years they have not gone further into track and field. It's a minefield of old traditions. IMG wanted to take the quickest way through it, the (Zola) Budd versus (Mary) Decker way, head-to-head races, just paying the superstars to race each other. But athletics is not just one race, it is a meeting of events, and the only way to progress it is the long way through the national governing bodies, building credibility and respect. This is not so much a criticism of IMG as an indication of the individualistic nature of the sport.

'There is always going to be a conflict between commercial and competitive areas, and there comes a point where an agent – manager says this is a good deal, right money, good image, take it, and a coach says you can't afford five days for a shoot in Mauritius. I've encountered that problem myself.'

So has Daley Thompson who did a hugely successful television commercial for the restorative drink Lucozade. When their advertising agency tried to sign him for a follow-up campaign the first days he felt he could offer them for their shoot without compromising his competitive priorities were a year away.

Coe has also steadfastly refused to compromise his preparations for a championship to accommodate races which might suit sponsors or television, a philosophy which has cost him money. Cram, who made more than £100,000 by his agent's own admission from competitive appearance fees in 1986, has been far more successful in that area, but Coe does not regret the course he took. 'Very early on I realized that getting the commercial foundations laid with long-term contracts with the right companies outside the sport meant that I would not be dependent on money from the track.It would mean that I would never be in a position in which I ran because I needed the money when I knew that it would be better if I did not run.

'The bulk of my money has not come from my sport. I freely admit that in that respect I am not in the income bracket of most athletes of my level of achievement. But the beauty of doing it my way is that even when my track days are behind me I will have contracts which continue to pay me. The contract with Diadora runs for four years beyond when I shall finish running and contracts like that have allowed me to plough my own path in athletics. I think it's been one of the reasons why I have never been out of the medals in any championship I have contested since 1977. My independence has paid off.'

Coe parted company with IMG after five years just before Christmas 1986, signing instead with Quilter Goodison, the London stockbroker and its offshoot, Faith, which is run by a friend of Coe, former pop-singer and actor Adam Faith. Faith is involved in portfolio management and Coe is the only person with whom he has a total career involvement. 'It just came out of our friendship,' says Coe. 'If somebody had said two or three years ago that I'd be closely associated with him, a show-business personality, I would have had to smile, but he is an extremely successful businessman who has passed his stockbroking exams. He has that streetwise sharpness but at the same time he understands top level performers, and the demands and pressures on them, because of his own experiences. It's not a normal agent – client relationship because it's broader, but then it's different anyway because we're friends.'

An example, says Coe, is Faith's attitude to his bid to become the first man to win the Olympic 1,500 metres for a third time in 1988, something to which he decided to devote one final year in the sport. 'He said to me, "If you think I'm going out to do business for you this year when there's something so much more important, you're wrong." He told me bluntly that if I wanted him to arrange commercial things in that year, I'd have to stop running. If not, he would keep the year clear. It's not how your normal agent would look at things.'

But it is an attitude that Coe himself has maintained since the abortive series with Ovett, and one which he believes is common to the most successful performers. The priority each year is an event, whether it is the Olympics for him, or the British Open for a golfer or Wimbledon. Everything else must be arranged around that objective.

The examples of performers who have slipped from the highest pinnacles of sport because they devoted too much time to business are legion. The most-often quoted case was that of golfer Tony Jacklin after he won the British and US Open titles. So far it has not happened in athletics but they may be only a question of time. Today's generation of superstars came into the sport when there was nothing but medals to be won; tomorrow's, who grew up hearing of the fortunes to be made, may have different ambitions.

Coe himself fears that the signs are there already. 'I do think that we may have helped create a monster,' he admits. 'The people of my generation still have it in perspective but maybe we've changed it for others, maybe we're leaving behind a world where competing for money becomes more important than an Olympic gold medal.'

In other sports it is a world which already exists. Standards decline, it would appear, as earnings rise. Tennis has seen fines for bad behaviour and bad language mount in proportion to the prize money and, arguably, as a result of it. England cricket captains abuse and intimidate umpires, racing drivers throw punches at each other and the conduct of footballers is so unbecoming that a record suspension had to be imposed during the 1987 – 8 weeks on a player sent off eleven times. Money may not be the root of all evil but when the consequence of losing is a pain in the pocket, playing the game is, inevitably, the first casualty. A sporting vocation has evolved into an occupational chore, as *The Times* said sadly in 1987.

What is available within Coe's own sport has grown enormously in five years. In 1985 Zola Budd was paid £90,000 to run against Mary Decker, who received £56,000. In 1987, a Spanish promoter paid over $70,000 to bring together the sprinters, Ben Johnson (then Commonwealth, later to be world champion), Carl Lewis (Olympic champion), Calvin Smith (world record holder) and Linford Christie (European champion) for a race which lasted barely ten seconds. The British Amateur Athletic Board, once the staunchest guardians of the amateur code, distributed a fifth of its income, more than £800,000, during a single year as enticements to athletes to appear in their sponsored and televised events. The javelin thrower Fatima Whitbread was paid £10,000 for each competition for just six throws, while there were clubs in the country holding jumble sales to raise the money to buy six javelins.

Such moral issues are Coe's to ponder now in his role as a vice-chairman of the Sports Council of England; a job which pays him an annual salary of £10,000 for devoting many of his spare hours to the sporting cause. 'The intellectual input of my week' is how he describes the work. 'It's probably the only normal job I've had unless you count being a research assistant at Loughborough University which kept me in food and paid my day-to-day expenses.'

The money it pays is irrelevant to him. He is not working for financial reasons, he says. 'I need the intellectual stimulation. Even in the years when running has been the priority, I've needed that. If I sat back and did nothing my athletics was the worse for it. Eight hours good sleep a night and something to challenge the mind as well as the body is a pretty good lifestyle.'

It leaves him little time for sitting back. He sits behind a vast mahogany desk in an office opposite London's Euston station, leather briefcase and diary to hand and all the appearance of a thrusting businessman. But you catch him where you can. In 1987, when an injury frustrated his hopes for the track, he was moving as smartly off the track as he would have wished to on it.

The diary recorded seven days in September, typical of many weeks that year, which began one Monday with a drive from his Thameside home in Twickenham to a breakfast meeting at London's Carlton Towers Hotel, and continued through the day with a meeting at the Sports Council, another with the Lawn Tennis Association and ended at 11pm that night after a six hour meeting with the Minister of Sport, Mr Colin Moynihan, at the Department of Environment.

The following day he was in Euston again for a 10am meeting at the Sports Council to discuss the affairs of the British Amateur Athletic Board and finished his day with a late afternoon discussion on his own business affairs at Faith's office in Knightsbridge. On Wednesday there was a breakfast television interview to give for TV-am on the subject of drugs in sports and another for a magazine, and then he drove to Guildford for a meeting at Diadora's British offices. On Thursday he devoted all morning to a photo-session for C & A ('and grabbed an afternoon off'), and on Friday he gave a press conference with the Minister of Sport on the drugs issue and recorded an interview for the BBC TV programme *Panorama*.

Saturday found him travelling to the Sports Council's centre at Plas-y-Brenin in North Wales for a Sunday and Monday strategy conference, and at 3pm on the Monday a friend flew him by helicopter from a nearby RAF station to a field behind his house in Essex so that he could be back at the Carlton Towers Hotel again by 6pm to star at the British launch of the Diadora's 1988 range. 'Somewhere along the line I fitted my training into the programme,' he adds.

It is all good practice, of course, for the 'after-life'; that void to be filled in every competitor's life when the last race has been run, the last ball struck and there are all those years ahead when another generation do not stop to ask for an autograph. For Coe the line will be crossed for the last time in the late summer of 1988 but already, characteristically, his plans are firmly laid. He will hardly break stride between the two lives. Coe, star runner of the Diadora range, will become Coe the chairman of Diadora (UK) Ltd.

'My father has always been a businessman, I grew up in a business environment, and I have a degree in economics, practically geared to business economics and finance. My brother, who had the inate ability for business I had for running, is a partner already in a retail group in designer clothing. It seemed logical for me to go into business as well.'

He had plenty of practice. While at Loughborough he had been involved in organizing a major track meeting, negotiating with television and sponsors, and he has enjoyed 'lots of talks with sponsors at the Sports Council'.

A re-negotiation of his Diadora contract offered the opportunity. Coe knew that Diadora were unhappy with their distribution in Britain. The company with the rights was under capitalized and little had been spent on advertising and promotion. So when his own endorsement contract was discussed, he opened the question of taking over the rights. 'It's not so strange that I should start owning a piece of the company I've been promoting. I'd worked closely with them. I'd been involved in improving their products. I wasn't just lending my name. I could see the potential.'

The deal Coe admits was not handed to him as a grace and favour for past service. 'It took hours of hard negotiations.' The Italians had to be convinced that Coe offered them the same return as a businessman that he did as an athlete but the commitment to set up – and invest in – a joint company, employing two other working directors who came from the previous distributors, sold it to them. He has two contracts with Diadora now, one for endorsement until 1992 and another as the chairman of a joint venture company.

In the first year, when he is running still, he will confine his involvement to overseeing an advertising campaign to the trade, promotions and company strategy; but in future, he says, 'the company will be my challenge'.

Certainly he will not feel the pinch when he stops competing. His motivation to succeed may never have been financial but for those who keep sport's fiscal score Coe has been one of the winners. When he gets his hands finally on the Trust Fund in his name, he could, as he says himself, 'live a comfortable, if not excessive, lifestyle without ever working again'.

Bob Woolf, with two of his star players – Bobby Orr (left), who played hockey for the Boston Bruins in the 1960s and 70s, and top basketball player, Larry Bird, of the Boston Celtics.

4

THE AMERICAN AGENT

FOR MOST of the first hundred years of organized sport, the professional sportsman survived without the services of an agent. No such person existed within the sporting arena, not would any have been tolerated by the clubs and associations which controlled the business of sport. The players drew the crowds but when they wanted the rate for the job they were on their own.

Professional sport was a feudal peonage and the player was little more than a serf in a sporting squirearchy owing his livelihood to the patronage of the lord of his manor. It was they, the entrepreneurs, promoters and club owners, who signed the deals, and the player who signed the autographs. On both sides of the Atlantic the professional player accepted what he was given for the privilege of playing the game he loved, and the owners of ball clubs and arenas closed ranks to exploit him to the full.

In England, the Football League prevented players from selling their services to the highest bidder for seventy-five years by using their monopoly of the professional game to impose a maximum wage upon them. As recently as 1960, the outstanding player in the English game could not be paid more than £20 a week, and then only during the playing season. In summer, when he rested on his laurels, he was paid only £17.

If the money was poor, the conditions of employment imposed were worse. During the same period, the professional cricketer was less highly regarded than amateurs in the same team, not because he was a lesser player but because he was considered a lesser person for accepting reward for his efforts. Most English county clubs refused to have a professional player as their captain and, until 1953, England chose not to. Indeed, at many grounds, professionals endured the indignity of being forced to use different changing rooms to the amateurs and entering the field of play through a different gate.

The situation was little different in the United States. Professional sports players there were marked out even from other workers by a decision of the Supreme Court in 1922 which excluded major league sport from the provisions of anti-trust legislation, not only allowing clubs to collude in fixing salary scales but also preventing players from becoming free agents when their contracts expired. Thus, salaries were kept artificially low. In 1960, no professional basketball player was earning more than $50,000 and the highest paid player in the National Football League did not make more than $30,000.

Negotiations on their terms were a one-sided contest between wily owner and grateful youth, and there was only one winner. For a player to seek specialist advice or to bring his lawyer with him to even up the odds, while not against any rule, would have been considered both disloyal and disrespectful. None dared. When one young half-back was so bold as to ask one-time San Francisco 49ers owner Tony Morabito whether he could discuss what he had been offered with his wife, Morabito replied: 'If you do, I'll have to call my wife and ask if it's okay to offer you that much'.

The agent first intruded into this private game in the United States at the beginning of the sixties, not by design but in the capacity of an attorney guiding a client through the complexities of the endorsement contracts the more famous players were being offered outside their sport.

The pioneers were loathe to use the word agent. Mark McCormack, a young Cleveland lawyer who was to create the International Management Group, the world's largest agency specializing in the representation of sportsmen and women, described himself in the early days as a sports attorney. Agent had connotations of the fast-talking, cigar-smoking Mr Ten Per Cents of Hollywood legend – and still has today. 'It's like saying you're a bank robber or a rapist,' says the lawyer David Falk, senior vice-president of ProServ Inc., an agency founded in Washington DC in 1969 by tennis player Donald Dell. Indeed, in 1987, two men calling themselves sports agents were targets of a Federal racketeering inquiry with claims that they threatened to break the legs of a sports star who wished to end his contract with them.

Yet it is this new professional class within sport that transformed the lot of the muddied oafs and flannelled fools of this world, and caused the pendulum to swing so far the other way that there are players in US basketball earning more than $2,000,000 from their clubs for a season's work and in Britain soccer players earning £2,000 a week.

Legal decisions both sides of the Atlantic which removed the restrictions on trade have made the new world possible, and competition to the sporting establishment for their services from rival leagues and foreign clubs has given the players a bargaining tool. But it is the advent of the agent which has enabled them to exploit their advantages. Agents, Peter Ueberroth, baseball's commissioner has said, are now the lords of the game.

Robert G. Woolf did not so much enter the business in 1964 as create a new part for himself. While McCormack, who had begun by offering advice to golfer Arnold Palmer in 1960, had chanced upon a specialization in individual competitors (at first only golfers) Woolf, from a similar legal background and as fortuitously, stumbled upon a role looking after the interests of the team men. A telescope pointing through a window of his office on the forty-fifth floor of the Prudential Tower in Boston is focused on the pitcher's mound at Fenway Park, home of the Boston Red Sox, and is a permanent reminder of where it began.

At the time, Woolf was a successful criminal lawyer in Boston, a 'defender of the guilty', as one district attorney called him, with a reputation for sweet-talking judges into uncharacteristic leniency. One miscreant he represented who admitted the theft of a $50,000 diamond-encrusted coffee pot (the property, as it happened, of the President of the United States) was chastised with nothing more severe than a term of probation. It was a persuasive skill that was to be Woolf's most important tool in his new career.

On his legal successes was built a practice which sustained eight lawyers and from which he enjoyed an income of $100,000. He had no reason to expect Earl Wilson's visit to his office, in November 1964, to change anything. 'It was a time in my life when I was open to new directions but I had no thoughts of representing people in sport, or in anything else but criminal matters. I can't say the thought had ever entered my head. It was just one of those things that happens to you.'

The Duke, as team-mates called Wilson, was the Red Sox's star right-handed pitcher, with a 'big fast ball and a live arm'. His 'office' was that mound at Fenway Park, but all he was seeking from Woolf was advice over an automobile accident and he had chosen him for no better reason than the proximity of the law firm's office to his home.

The advice proffered, the two men got talking about sport, a mutual interest since, as Woolf told Wilson proudly, 'I've played a bit of ball myself'. In fact, he had been good enough as a teenager to win an athletic scholarship to the respected Boston College; a Jewish lad talented enough to be sought to play basketball in a Jesuit college. The old jock and young pro found a natural affinity. Soon Wilson was a regular visitor at Woolf's home and was entrusting his tax affairs and the arrangement of his personal appearances to him – and other Red Sox players asked for introductions.

The help he could give Wilson and his friends was confined to their off-field activities, the small number of personal appearances they made, and to making sure that the best earning years of their lives were not devoted to supporting the Inland Revenue Service. There was never any thought given to acting for them in their negotiations with the Boston club.

Indeed, it was two years before Woolf entered negotiations with one of his clients' employers, and again it was Wilson who enabled him to make the break through for all players in American team sport when he asked him for help in negotiations with the management of his new club, Detroit Tigers. The help had to be limited: Woolf, the two men decided, should not be present during the negotiations in the office of Tigers' general manager Jim Campbell for fear that Wilson would be seen as a radical troublemaker. Woolf had to remain at a discreet distance.

He never actually left his hotel room. Wilson went alone to

meet Campbell, armed with Woolf's detailed advice about the terms he should ask for, and only when there was disagreement did Wilson excuse himself on the grounds of a call of nature to make a call to seek Woolf's opinion on the tactics to adopt. Finally, a deal was struck. Campbell may have wondered about the state of his pitcher's bladder but he was talked into one of the game's first deferred-compensation agreements which spread Wilson's earnings and, consequently, his tax burden far beyond the end of his career. He repaid Tigers handsomely during the next season by winning twenty-two games and launched Woolf into a new business. Within five years Woolf had left criminal work to others and his company, Robert G. Woolf Associates, was representing more than 300 clients in face-to-face negotiations with general managers of sport.

It was not surprising that a man accustomed to standing before judges found the front men of ball clubs less awesome than his clients did, but Woolf knew also that he had an innate ability for horse trading. Doing a deal, as he admits, gives him a 'buzz'. He was eight when he went into business for the first time, delivering newspapers in his home town of Portland, Maine ($1 a week per house), and at sixteen, when he was old enough to qualify for a driver's licence, he had founded the Woolf Supply Company of New England which bought from factories and sold to stores from the back of a twelve-year-old 'heap' packed so full that the doors were held closed with rope.

It was at that early age, facing the shopkeepers of Boston, that Woolf first understood the psychology of the salesman, of talking judges into soft sentences and owners into generous contracts. 'I've never made a demand in my life, not in any of the negotiations I've done,' he says. 'I suggest, I ask: "Is this something you can live with?" That way nobody feels they are being hustled. The suggestion's there and it grows on them but nobody is forced into anything. I don't want the people I do business with to feel bad about what they've agreed.'

Far from earning him the reputation of a soft touch, the magazine *Newsweek* once commented that 'rich and authoritative franchise owners shudder at the mere snap of the lock on his attaché case'. Many of the contracts he has negotiated for players have earned them enough for a lifetime in a single year. Seventeen of his clients earned at least $1 million from their club contracts during 1987 and, when he negotiated Larry Bird's current contract with Boston Celtics in 1983, he achieved for him the status of the highest paid team player in the world.

Woolf's office is a shrine to the deals he has done and the men for whom he struck them. A huge basketball boot, three feet from toe to heel, sits on a low table, a present from the Converse company after Woolf negotiated a multi-million dollar, multi-year endorsement contract with them for Bird. There is a Spalding basketball as a reminder of a similar deal he did for Bird with that company, and shelves of other mementoes; the playing kit of grateful clients, pictures of Woolf with his stars and a whole wall devoted to the career of Carl Yastrzemski, whose batting led the Red Sox to the 1975 World Series. 'The day he was finishing playing, he asked me to clear his locker room of all the souvenirs, everything he had been given over the years, all just left there. So during the game I paid two ball boys to pack it into the trunk of my car, and after the game Yaz says, 'it's yours, the lot.' That's it, on the wall, the start of my collection.'

Woolf has represented many of the greatest names in American team sport: basketball's Bird, Otis Birdsong and John Havlicek; football's Jim Plenkett, Joe Theismann and John Matuszak; baseball's Ken Harrelson and Yastrzemski, and ice hockey's Derek Sanderson, once the highest paid professional athlete in the world. One usually led to another. Recommendations by word of mouth are Woolf's only advertisements. He was never an ambulance-chaser as an attorney and, since he came into what he calls 'the sports-representation business', he has not hung around ball parks seeking business. As far as Woolf is concerned, it has always been appointment by invitation only.

Others are less scrupulous. World Sport and Entertainment Inc, a company which came into sport from the pop music industry, have admitted paying top college players to sign contracts with them. The father of David Robinson, the number one draft choice in 1987 for the National Basketball Association, revealed that two agents 'tried to bribe us' to sign with them. The checks he made on potential representatives before his son chose the agency Advantage International to represent him would have satisfied the CIA. 'You have to be fortunate enough to find somebody who is honest,' says Los Angeles Raiders defensive end Howie Long. 'Let's face it, an axe murderer could be an agent in today's sport.'

In Britain, where there are few indigenous agencies, there are proportionately as many ready to take the money off the unwary athlete. One who represented several athletes, including Olympic champion Allan Wells, went to prison for four years for fraud. He caused some of his clients to lose five-figure sums.

In America, where, as Woolf says, 'there are more so-called professional agents than there are profesisonal athletes', the most renowned and sought-after athletes are so spoiled for choice that they can afford to be as selective over their personal representative as they are over the club they will represent. Before the young Larry Bird appointed him, Woolf submitted to two long interviews by the senior citizens of the Indiana town of Terra Hawk who were advising their most famous son.

Indeed, Woolf was just one of many agents who attended the first series of interviews. His lasted eight hours, and Bird was never present. Only at a second interview, after Woolf had been short-listed, did he meet the player for the first time.

'All the talking was done by these local guys. Larry said nothing. After a couple of hours, I was going over salaries of top baseball players, Reggie Jackson, Jim Rice and the like, and suddenly one guy says "hey, how about Tommy Johns". He was a pitcher with the Yankees who came from Terra Hawk. Now everybody is saying yes, hey, how about that, what does Tommy make. And the first words Larry Bird says to me are "Mr Woolf" – and he still calls me Mr Woolf even now we are neighbours – "Tommy Johns happens to be a friend of mind and I don't wish to know what he makes." I couldn't believe the integrity of such a young man. I was proud to be asked to represent such a man.'

Conversely, a reputable agent has to guard his own reputation jealously from certain players. Woolf admits to having refused to represent some and to have shown others the door once he came to know them. 'I can smell someone who's going to be trouble, and then it doesn't matter how good they are at sport.' He recalls one of the best players in American sport today who was once a client. 'First contract I got him he spent $245,000 in three weeks on himself; furs, jewellery, a trip to Hawaii, all the ego business.

We went our different ways.'

There are other rules of engagement that Woolf insists that his clients respect. The most important is the sanctity of a contract. Too many in his experience have thought that a contract was a piece of paper binding only on others. Woolf lost major clients Julius Erving and John Matuszak because they wanted to re-negotiate their contracts for more money when in the middle of great seasons. 'Would you re-negotiate for less if you were having a bad season?' Woolf asked them. When a rival company offered more for Bird's signature before his contract with Converse was in writing, Woolf turned them down. 'I don't think it's old-fashioned to keep your word,' he says.

He also believes that clients should not be present during nego-tiations with their employers. 'That way there is never any animosity left over from the negotiating between them and their clubs. They haven't been involved. If the management say that what I have asked is outlandish, that it's out of the question, it's me who has asked too much, not their player,' he says.

Most clients are so trusting that they do not ask how negotia-tions are progressing, 'They say "let me know when you think the contract is fair"'. Some put absolute trust in Woolf to handle their affairs. Theismann, quarter-back for the Washington Redskins, did it without ever meeting Woolf. They met for the first time by chance at a Washington reception after Theismann's retirement. Woolf, in return, never asks for anything in writing from his clients. 'Do you have a contract with your lawyer?' he asks. 'It's a matter of trust and if that doesn't exist between two people, what good's a signature on paper?'

Representatives have come into the business by fixing individual deals for players without representing them in any formal capacity, selling the idea of an appearance by the player to a company in the hope that later the player can be persuaded to fulfil the engagement. The profit is in the mark-up of the middle man rather than in a fixed percentage. McCormack, a fine amateur golfer himself, who was an acquaintance of Arnold Palmer and Gary Player, began that way and did so well on the golfers' behalf that they asked him to manage all their affairs.

That involves a far more comprehensive package, doing every-thing possible to ensure that a client is able to concentrate on his game. It is resource management, both sides doing what they are best at. 'If a man's mind isn't on the game, he isn't so valuable to the team and then he isn't as valuable to me,' says Woolf. So no detail is too trivial. A client will be reminded that his wife's birthday is imminent. Will he buy the present or does he wish the agency to handle it? Woolf had one client who asked his office to have his car collected. 'All he could remember was that it was in Michigan. Somewhere,' says Randy Vataha, Woolf's chief operating officer and a former receiver himself with the New England Patriots. 'We've even settled domestic arguments.'

Woolf is always available. Players can phone him toll-free from anywhere in the United States on a special number. They also have his mobile phone number. 'When it's not going right for a player, it's not enough for someone to be saying "don't worry" because that goes in one ear and out the other,' says Vataha. 'It's another thing for somebody with years of experience to tell you history, how it happened this way for other guys and how it worked out for them, and then you feel you are not on your own out there. Whatever happened when I was a player, I called Bob – if I was down, call Bob. If I wasn't playing well, call Bob. Bob's been in sport so long there's nothing that could happen that he has not experienced.'

The package amounts to three related responsibilities – making money, managing it and, crucially, protecting the client from the dangers of having it. The first is paramount but a representative failing to take care of the other responsibilities is failing a client. 'In the end, our aim, the whole purpose of our work, is to set a player up for life, or at least as far as his talent makes it possible for us to,' says Woolf.

That is a crucial difference between representation in show business and the sports business. An actor or actress, given the talent, has a lifetime of work ahead. The most talented sporting competitor has, at most, about ten years at the top and few will continue to receive anywhere near their peak earnings from the day they retire from the field. Racing driver Jackie Stewart and tennis player Bjorn Borg are exceptions because their renown goes beyond the sporting arena, but such men are rarer still among the team sports.

In a team sport, a player will have probably one, and certainly not more than two chances of concluding a playing contract generous enough to guarantee the future beyond the day he hangs up his boots. For a lucky few, the chance comes almost before they have proved they can produce the goods. Woolf negotiated a $8.2 million contract with Tampa Bay Buccaneers for the 22-year-old Vinny Testaverde which will earn him money for twelve years. And he managed this before the college quarterback had played a single professional game.

It is the negotiating with the owners and general managers that Woolf enjoys most and it is the principal reason why he has never locked horns with men like McCormack and Dell for the representation of the famous in individual sports, even though that decision has limited his business to North America. 'The expertise of this company lies primarily in negotiation, and you cannot negotiate for people in individual sports where they get paid only for winning,' he says.

Woolf could not have had any idea whether Testaverde was a winner when he was asked by the young man's father to handle his affairs, because he had never seen him play, but his own subjective opinion of playing ability is irrelevant anyway to a client's value. How much a club needs him is far more influential on the eventual bottom line, and Woolf knew Tampa Bay needed Testaverde badly. They were the least successful team in the National Football League the previous season and their owner, Hugh Culverhouse, a 67-year-old tax attorney, was desperate to shake life into a franchise with a losing record.

In one respect Testaverde's selection as the NFL's number one draft – the most coveted player coming out of the colleges – was a disadvantage. Tampa, as the least successful club in 1986, were guaranteed the number one draft choice and Woolf could not negotiate with any other NFL club. There was only one angle for him to exploit. Tampa had had the number one draft choice the previous year – again in 1985 they had been the least successful club – but that player had decided instead to accept an offer from a baseball club, a serious embarrassment to Culverhouse and something he would not wish to happen again.

So Woolf met Culverhouse to sell him the University of Miami's most valuable player. In the old days Culverhouse's wealth and experience would have intimidated a young college boy and certainly his father, a labourer, but a meeting of two attorneys was a meeting of equals, and, as *Time* magazine had said of Woolf: 'If the athlete of today has become what the movie star of yesterday was, then Bob Woolf is the Cecil B. DeMille of the locker room.'

Woolf had decided the bottom line in his own mind. 'Vinny was the number one draft, so you start by asking for at least as much as any rookie ever got.' Woolf once arrived at a figure of $500,000-a-year as the value of ice hockey player Derek Sanderson simply because he had read that the world's highest paid team player at the time was soccer's Pele who was on $400,000. 'It doesn't ever hurt to ask because no club will say yes if they can't handle it.'

When he suggested $8 million to Culverhouse the owner did not say yes immediately but he must have been aware from that first meeting that he was going to have to unlock the vaults to sign his man. The negotiations continued in half-a-dozen phone calls between Woolf and Culverhouse before, finally, Culverhouse agreed. At that point Woolf offered to spread the six-year salary over twelve years to help Culverhouse's cash flow – and his client's tax position – in return for more money to cover the loss on inflation and investment. The contract was signed and the highest-paid rookie in NFL history met the owner for the first time.

Whether Tampa and Culverhouse can afford such a salary for one player, Woolf does not regard as his concern. 'They could have said no,' he points out. 'You cannot blame agents or players for a lot of clubs in today's leagues losing money. The people to blame are owners. They've been fiscally irresponsible for years. They are into this ego thing about owning a ball club. All they want is their name in the papers, to be a celebrity. So they've thrown the money around, and you can't blame the players for picking it up.'

Not that the salaries of players such as Testaverde will force Culverhouse to haul his belt in a notch. *Forbes* magazine listed him in 1987 as one of America's 400 wealthiest people with a personal fortune of $250 million. Seven others who owned all or part of the franchises of NFL clubs were also among that number. But it is not a business guaranteed to increase those fortunes.

Most franchises lose money and Vataha had personal experience of that. He bought the New England franchise in the new United States Football League with the profits he made from a chain of racketball clubs, and lost money on the deal. Few have shown much concern for losses because the price of their ego trip can be set against taxes; but if any introduced the business methods that made them their fortunes in other areas, sport might feel the pinch.

Already Woolf can foresee the good days ending. 'How can it last? There are fifty-six players in baseball making more than $1 million in 1987, and the rest are mad because they don't make a million. It can't last like that, not for long. It doesn't fit within the economics of the sport. Already we've seen the American Basketball Association, the World Football League and the World Hockey Association disappear because salaries reached unrealistic levels. It will happen again and that must concern us because it is not in the interest of our clients for leagues to fold up. But it's up to the owners to say enough, no more.'

The contract Woolf negotiated for Testaverde ensures that Tampa will have to pay Testaverde whether or not he plays for them, and however well he performs when he does – unusual in a game in which the average player has little contract security because of a clause in the typical NFL contract which allows clubs to cut their staff at any time. Only an outstanding player, such as Testaverde, can negotiate such a clause out of his contract, but Woolf himself is opposed to performance-related bonuses, the extras for yardage gained, home runs hit and goals scored. 'All a player thinks about then is their bonus, not the team, and if they are doing that it hurts both of us because I have a lesser ball player to negotiate for.'

There was another, non-fiscal reason for Woolf to offer the club a contract spread over twelve years: a player paid over twelve years cannot spend his millions so fast. 'There isn't so much there, so there isn't so much temptation,' says Vataha. 'He has a good standard of living and we have the chance to create good spending habits.'

Testaverde's monthly salary cheques are paid directly to Woolf's office which has power of attorney over their distribution. The player is paid an agreed allowance. Bird, whose income from salary and endorsements exceed $4 million, has such modest personal needs that he spends only $10,000 annually himself.

Each client has a monthly budget prepared, their wills written, trusts planned, corporate structures organized and taxation settled. Investments are advised upon by Professional Planners Inc, a sister corporation of Woolf's run by Bob Shaughnessy, a former captain of Harvard football team and former Merrill Lynch executive. Their philosophy is conservative. Woolf's proudest claim is that they have never lost a nickel of a client's money. Vataha learned his lesson from a friend who earned only $60,000 dollars a year as a player but was persuaded to put all his savings into a high-flying Californian company called Technical Equities. He lost $300,000 when it went down. So Woolf looks for security more than a high return. 'Sports players don't get a second chance to earn money,' he says. 'If they lose it, they've lost it forever. Better ten per cent return than a risky twenty per cent.'

Not that Testaverde will want for many luxuries. Jill Leone, Woolf's executive vice-president and former secretary, who handles all endorsements and appearance negotiations, tied up some immediate deals to make his life in Tampa more comfortable. One, with Chevrolet, provided Testaverde with a Corvette to drive (when he was not using his own Jaguar), and another with a boat dealership gave him a $150,000 powerboat to play with off the Florida coast.

But having made his client the money, and managed it, Woolf also believes in protecting the client from it. 'Fame often precedes maturity,' he likes to say. He was quick to phone Testaverde on hearing that he was planing to fly to Atlantic City to watch a big fight there. 'I don't like a young player thinking he can go here, there and everywhere because he has money.'

Advice is part of the service. What is 'right' for the client is important, not only as a player, but as a marketable commodity. McCormack admits to having 'discussed' with the French skier Jean-Claud Killy whether he should marry the woman he was living with at a time when his marketable image was as an eligible bachelor. Woolf says bluntly: 'I'm not intimidated by any of my clients. If I haven't got the experience to advise them why are they hiring me? I may risk losing them but my job, as long as they are hiring me, is to tell the truth. I'm not paid to say "oh, sure, wonderful, you're the superstar, you do what you want, it must be right." If he thinks a client has let his team down in a game he will say so. 'If I heard one was on drugs I'd phone the coach and tell him we have a problem, let's work it out together because it's in both our interests.'

Woolf rides shotgun on clients like a guard running protection for a quarter-back, or, as he would prefer to consider it, a father keeping an eye on a teenage son. In many respects, Woolf, and all agents, are acting in locum parentis. Team players are usually younger than the individual sports stars other agents represent, and they have been part of a team, in high school, college and now professionally where everything has been done for them as long as they can remember. They may be big men physically but emotionally many are babes in arms.

In the early days Woolf had clients who went with girls who later threatened them with a rape accusation unless they were paid. ('And it didn't happen just once.') Now players are briefed on the dangers, and how to respond, and when they travel to other cities they are warned of those likely to invite them to parties or offer them deals. Woolf's golden rule to all is 'if you are offered something for nothing, run, because it will cost you. 'Even now I get calls at all hours from guys who've just been offered this amazing deal for $5,000, and what should he do? I always say the same: sleep on it.'

'All my clients are clean-cut. It's a family, the people working for me, the people they are working for. I have three children. I've tried to bring them up right, show them the right way and then trust them. I always say that at 5.05 they were good but I can't vouch for them at six. It's the same with clients. I just hope I've set them up so that when they meet people they will be a good example.'

With a player as famous and as popular as Bird, most of an agency's time is spent, as Vataha puts it, 'keeping Larry as private as he wants to be'. They get fifteen calls a day offering Bird work or asking him to make appearances. Most he never hears about because the agency rejects them. Some will be 'run past him' for non-fiscal reasons, such as his public persona. Woolf always advises clients to be seen putting something back, perhaps giving a scholarship to an alma mater, making a donation to a project in their old community or giving game tickets to children. 'They should prepare themselves for the future, for the time when they are not the number one guy.' Occasionally the agency will propose a client for a project because it will be good for that image, as Leone did when she proposed Bird to an advertising agency looking for a famous name to improve the corporate image of the Raytheon conglomerate in a television commercial.

Woolf negotiates about 100 contracts a year. He concluded a $250,000 book deal for himself recently to write on the art of negotiation. 'I could negotiate a contract every day but we have to be able to look after the people which is what takes the time,' he says. With a staff of only twenty, including secretaries, there has to be limits.

For all Woolf's company does for clients, he charges a maximum fee of five per cent, and not five per cent of everything he negotiates but only on earned income, an important distinction in a sport such as football where very few players have guaranteed employment. Other agencies with team players charge their percentage up front, arguing that they made the deal, it's up to the player to make the team. So if a player is on a $1 million four-year contract and is cut after one season, he has earned only $250,000 while the agent has taken five per cent of a million. Woolf, moreover, does not regard his five per cent as low, even though in individual sports such as golf and tennis ten per cent and even twenty per cent is common. 'It would be low for the entertainment industry but for sport, it's reasonable.'

Certainly it keeps him in as much luxury as any of his players. He lives in Boston, with his wife Anne, two daughters and a son he hopes will move into the 'family business'. He keeps apartments in Washington and Los Angeles, a summer home on Cape Cod and a winter retreat in Florida; and drives cars which do not merge into the background. But drop by and it is most likely you will find yourself doing nothing more extravagant than playing ball on his private basketball court.

He sees nothing dishonourable about making that living off the sweated labour of sportsmen, any more than there was in defending criminals. 'There's nothing dishonest about being a sports agent. Thirty per cent of sports agents in the United States are attorneys, and they have the ethics committee of the American Bar Association watching over them.' Most agents he knows are enjoying the combination of business with pleasure. McCormack, asked whether he would give up everything if he could have been US Open Champion, admitted: 'It would be a close call.' Woolf says: 'I live a Walter Mitty existence. I sometimes ask God, why me? Nobody could have a better life.'

Woolf's own reputation is such that he has even represented Admiral Stansfield Turner, the former head of the CIA. Indeed there are only two professions he will not represent. Boxers are one. Howard Cossell, a television personality who made his name commentating on boxing, warned him off them. Rabbis are the other. He did represent one. His own. The man came to him for help when his synagogue would not give him a rise. Eight months of negotiations with their committee followed. Finally, he was able to tell the rabbi that he had negotiated a new three-year contract at a considerably increased salary. What he did not tell him was that he had achieved it only by making a large donation himself to the synagogue. 'No more rabbis,' he says.

Conquering the world of snooker – Barry Hearn (second from right) with four of the snooker players he manages: (from left) Steve Davis, Neal Foulds, Cliff Thorburn and Willie Thorne at the launch of their own Matchroom League.

5

THE MANAGER

BARRY HEARN must have led a sheltered childhood. The first snooker club he entered was one he owned. 'Never knew they existed,' he says. 'It wasn't my game.' It is now, almost lock, stock and the cue ball. Like on some magical table, or when Steve Davis is playing, the balls just kept dropping for him until he was the top man. What he does not control he takes a percentage from.

If it is luck to be the man in the right place at the right time, Hearn was very lucky. Snooker was a game of the clubs – the gentlemen's and the working men's, and of smokey, back-street halls – a game which was played by the masses but raised nobody's emotions. To be good at it was said to be a sign of a misspent youth. There was little purpose in it because there was little money in it.

Joe Davis had been world champion for as long as any devotee could remember and nobody outside the game could name another player, unless it was his brother Fred. To most men, it wasn't a sport but a game for winter evenings, like darts or bridge or shove ha'penny.

Hearn, at the age of twenty-six, bought into it because he saw the old halls as a property investment. They were in city centres with development potential, and he was the young finance director of an investment company looking to make a killing.

The company he persuaded his company to buy in 1974 was Lucania Temperance Billiard Halls (London) Ltd. It was a company with Welsh, turn of the century, origins when it owned the

91

three-table clubs in which miners played of an evening, but it had changed its name when it bought the fittings of the SS *Lucania* which sank in the Mersey.

There were eighty-six clubs at one time but without drinking licences clubs could not make three tables pay their way and the smallest had gone long before Hearn moved in. They were ripe for redevelopment but 1974 was the year the bottom fell out of the property market, so suddenly snooker looked a better bet. At least, in the short term. The investment company made Hearn chairman of the re-named Lucania Snooker Clubs, and quietly he began to buy a share of the investment company. When finally they sold, it was to make him a rich man.

There was no business background in his family. Hearn's father drove London Transport buses until he died of a heart-attack in his forties, and young Hearn did not set out to be a businessman. 'I started out wanting to make money because I was a working class lad who saw people in big houses and wanted a big house for myself.'

It was one of the reasons he never went to snooker halls. He was too busy swotting. But he loved sport. He can still remember the emotional tug he felt when Lillian Board was beaten by that French girl in the Mexico Olympics. 'I tried anything and failed at just about everything,' he says. 'What I had in enthusiasm I lacked in talent.'

He chose accountancy because you did not need to have money, but only to work hard. He started on a tiny salary under articles, studying nights and weekends because he could not afford to pay the fees a second time round if he failed. 'It taught me values,' he says. 'I don't pass up on anything now.' Growing up in working-class Dagenham also taught him his 'streetwise philosophy' of giving the customer value for money.

After completing his articles he went to accountants Thomson McLintock in the City for three years and then he answered an advertisement for an investment company seeking a finance director. He was still in his twenties when he became chairman of Lucania Snooker Clubs, and moved his office from North Kensington to the thirteen-table snooker club in Romford.

A Belfast boy called Alex Higgins, who played the game so fast they called him Hurricane, had won the world championships a year or two earlier, and television was putting on a series of games called *Pot Black*. In 1975, for the first time the odd hour from the world championships had been screened and there was a small rise in the graph of the game's popularity at the time. 'But nobody made any money at the game,' says Hearn. 'You could book any-body for £100 for the whole night.'

He had been in Romford four months when the club manager came into his office one day and asked him to come out to look at a player who wanted to play in the Lucania clubs' tournament. 'We put them on to encourage people into the clubs,' explains Hearn. 'They were only for amateurs.'

The player he saw on table thirteen was a tall, ginger-haired kid, pale and a bit puny, who said he was eighteen and could play a bit. 'He was so shy he barely said a word to me for a year,' says Hearn. 'I never gave a thought to managing him.' What he did give him was some work, playing the odd game as the 'good local kid' against a visiting professional at one of the clubs for £25.

That callow youth was Steve Davis, later to be world champion but then just one of the good amateurs Hearn gave work to in order to draw people into his clubs. Geoff Foulds, whose son Neal is now one of the eight world-class players Hearn manages, was another who was paid £25 for a lunch-time or evening's play after he won one of the Lucania tournaments. 'I wasn't managing them,' Hearn says. 'I was using them to market the clubs. It was the clubs I was interested in.' Several more of those he now manages played in those early amateur tournaments.

The next summer Hearn gave Davis a car and sent him round his clubs on a rota basis playing six hours in each. Players who fancied their chances against the young hopeful would come along and so would their friends. Davis was good for business. Hearn paid him some money, which Davis called a wage ('about £30 or £40,' Davis recalls) but Hearn says that he never legally employed him. 'He was sponsored, if you like,' he says. 'He could go off and do exhibitions in the evening if it suited him.' It was Davis' first taste of being a professional.

The big money in snooker play was in the betting. Hearn would get a call from a club owner in Leeds to send 'your boy' to play his champion. The fee for Davis would hardly cover the cost of the trip but it was experience for him and Hearn made a bit on the side betting on him. Davis himself didn't even make that because he has never gambled. When Davis won his first United Kingdom title in 1980, his prize was £6,000. Hearn made £6,500 backing him. 'We couldn't have made enough at times to cover our petrol, without gambling,' says Hearn.

The fortunes were in the future. In 1978 Hearn took Davis on a tour of clubs, anywhere that would give them a game: Leeds, Manchester, Blackpool. It was at that Lancashire seaside resort, at a bus-stop, that Hearn got him to sign a management contract. 'People who knew me were surprised that a guy making the money I was, as a company chairman, would want to know. Where's the money in it, they'd ask. But I'd always loved sport, competition. I'd watch anything. We had fun, became friends and I enjoyed myself. I could see something of myself in him. He wanted to be someone, and he was willing to make the sacrifices. I could associate with it.'

Still he did not think it was anything more than a pleasant diversion from mainstream business. He was on twenty per cent of Davis' money but in his first year as a professional Davis made only £5,481. 'And that was gross, before all his expenses. Let's be fair, it wasn't a living. He was having to live off his mum and dad.'

Then, in 1979, the Welshman Terry Griffiths won the world championships, and the game took off almost overnight, as though the public had been just waiting for somebody to light the touchpaper of a new national obsession. 'Television and the world championships changed how people saw the game,' says Hearn, but he does not claim to have anticipated it. It was a year later when Davis won the UK title and then the world title ('best he's ever played') that it came home to him. 'I thought, handled properly, this person and this game could be massive.'

Today it is, and Davis and Hearn are the most massive part of it. Since 1980, when prize money was £200,000, the graph of snooker's rise has been vertical. There were more than 400 hours of it on television in 1985. The early rounds of the Fidelity tournament in the autumn of 1987 was watched by more viewers than the final day's play when Britain's golfers won the Ryder Cup. In the 1986–7 season Davis himself won more than £250,000 in prizes, and teenage kids like Foulds and Steve Hendry were popping up with talent as though snooker was part of the national curriculum.

Davis recalls the growth. 'I was excited when Barry said my fee was up from £500 to £1,000 for a night and I remember my dad thinking it was brilliant the first time I got paid £3,000 for nine frames. He said it would have taken him nine months to earn that. But I've long since stopped looking at how many noughts there are because it's silly money.'

Davis was the only player Hearn managed until 1981 when Tony Meo joined him. Terry Griffiths came next and then Willie Thorn, Dennis Taylor, Foulds, Jimmy White and Cliff Thorburn. All, since Davis, have approached Hearn, although he knew all of them as friends or acquaintances. Taylor, the jovial Irishman distinguished by his square, up-side glasses, joined the team after winning the world championships by beating Davis on the last black.

He was managed by his wife at the time, an arrangement most players have when it involves nothing more than keeping their diary. A world champion needs more. Davis urged Hearn to approach Taylor. 'He needs you,' said Davis, but for ten days Hearn did nothing. Then the two met at a snooker occasion.

'We were mates, not close, but mates,' says Hearn. 'I said to him "I suppose I've got to manage you." ' 'I thought you were never going to ask,' said Taylor. 'I'm not asking,' said Hearn. 'Well I am,' said Taylor.

White, an exciting and volatile Londoner, as probably the second most sought-after player in the game, came to him after his former manager had approached Hearn to buy out his managerial contract. Hearn refused. 'I'm not in the business of buying people.' Later White phoned to say that he had bought out his manager's contract himself. 'Now are you interested?'

The deal is the same for all, twenty per cent of everything they make goes to Barry Hearn Ltd but all they have to do for themselves is play. Hearn organizes everything else, from marking up their diaries to filling in their tax returns.

'Don't call me an agent,' he says, pleadingly. 'I hate people calling me Mr Ten Cent.' For one thing, they would be selling him short, of course, but that is not his point. 'Agent's are percentage men. They do a deal, take their slice and that's the end of their interest. I take a percentage because that's the simplest way to decide my value, but I'm being paid for being a manager, a counsellor, an educationalist, an investment adviser, accountant, personal assistant and sometimes even driver. I do the deals but I handle the after-care as well. And most of all, I'm their friend. If they wouldn't be welcome in my house, they wouldn't be welcome in my team.'

In 1982, management became his full-time concern. It was not a deliberate move. He was still running the snooker clubs, and making good money doing it but Riley Leisure offered him a great deal of money and he says he does not believe in turning down great deals of money. 'It was the first time I had seen a cheque that big,' he says.

If work had still been only about money and big houses, Barry Hearn would have retired to enjoy the fruits. There is only so much a son of a London bus driver can spend and the £3.4 million Riley Leisure paid for the sale of sixteen snooker clubs more than covered it. But there was another motivation. He was enjoying himself. 'Snooker had started as a business and become my sport.'

So as part of his deal with Riley Leisure he kept the Romford club and the area within it called the Romford Matchroom, where Davis had played those early games against professionals. 'Part nostalgia but also good business because Romford makes money, and anyway it's a convenient base because I live only five miles up the road.'

He transformed Matchroom into a luxurious and private club with an exclusive membership of 200, most of them friends, where his professionals could relax among people they knew and Hearn would put up a £1,000 prize for a day's competition. 'Members would stay to four in the morning to see who won,' he says.

He also borrowed the name for a private management company, with its present staff of nine including two drivers, which operates all the activities of the eight players. Hearn and his two children are the directors, but the players are the Matchroom team. Two or three times a year they have management meetings to decide policy. They have decided major issues such as investing Matchroom money into co-promoting the launch of a World Series and creating the Matchroom League, and minor matters of style, like the wearing of dinner suits at afternoon as well as the evening sessions of tournaments. 'After all, viewers watching recordings in Hong Kong don't know that it's afternoon,' explains Hearn.

He has an influence on decisions but the group as a whole take them and then act as one. They have decided in the past not to play in a certain tournament ('or it may be against a certain player') and how Matchroom players should vote on an issue in the World Professional Billiards and Snooker Association, the game's governing body. Everything is done as a team and if a player objected so strongly to any decision that he could not go along with it, he would have to leave Matchroom.

More surprisingly, last year, the eight decided that it was no longer appropriate to gamble. Most of them had gambled. Some had had to in order to keep going in the early days. Now, they agreed, it was not good for the image of the team. Hearn went along with the majority.

The team is everything, except when it comes to playing each other. That's different. But away from the table, they work as a team, endorse as a team and represent sponsors as a team.

There are the Matchroom slippers (by Pirelli), the Matchroom aftershave (by Goya), the Matchroom Mob recordings (with London stars Chas and Dave), even a Matchroom duvet and, more naturally, Matchroom snooker tables. Soon there will be the Matchroom Country Club in Spain ten miles from Marbella where the team will be on a percentage of profits.

Davis has a private deal with the brewers Courage which dates back to 1982. Since 1984 he has been paid £200,000 a year for forty appearances on the company's behalf. It was hailed as snooker's first million-pound contract. 'He can be asked to do almost anything for them,' says Hearn. 'Play golf with them, open one of their clubs, dine with their bankers, play snooker with their customers. He's game for anything.'

And he is good at it. His public persona is far from accurate. He may be boringly efficient in tournament play, cold and calculating, but playing amateurs, or giving exhibitions of his trick shots, he is the life of the party, full of tales and wisecracks. 'His attitude, approach and behaviour are an example to any aspiring sportsman,' says Courage PR director Mike Reynolds.

Hearn has worked on it. He has directed the show like the man with the top hat and the big whip. 'My players realize that they've been given the keys to the chocolate factory and while it lasts they are going to enjoy it. And they are going to do their best to see it does last by getting the image right, the attitudes, looking good, being professional. Like their decision not to gamble, and to wear dinner jackets.

'Too many sportsmen think they can do what they like because it is their life. It isn't. The day they agree to be a professional sportsman they agree to share their lives. It is naive of them to think they can be a completely private person. If they want that they should find some other way of earning a fortune. We have a rule at Matchroom that we don't go home until the last autograph is signed. You may be there until two in the morning but that's fine. You owe it to those people. It's they who are paying you. And if you always treat the customer right, he will keep coming back. It pays dividends.'

Hearn is big on the customer. It's part of his streetwise philosophy. Market forces. Give value and be paid the rate. 'People want to be entertained and they want to be given value for the entrance fee they've paid. Isn't that true of everything in the eighties? It doesn't matter whether it is sport or industry. People have the money. If you give them what they want they'll pay the proper price for it.'

Hearn's price is high. Davis' daily fee is £5,000. Hearn is making a thousand every time Davis goes to work. Willie Thorn's is £2,000. 'It's all according to what the market will pay. The rate is what the market will pay for what a player does best – playing snooker. That's the rate we ask when they do anything else.'

In the early days Hearn would have Davis going from Newcastle to Devon overnight for £1,000. Now he might say that Davis is available between twelve and two. 'If somebody's willing to pay the price we won't turn down the work. That would be an insult to money, and that after all is the purpose of working, isn't it? But the price today reflects what the market will pay and obviously when you're charging what Steve does, fewer people will pay it. It suits him. He's happier playing snooker.'

Davis does not know what he is worth, or want to know. Hearn says that he has difficulty sitting Davis or White down to tell them. "Am I doing okay?" they say, and when I say fine, that's OK with them. The difference between £350,000 and £400,000 is unimportant to them. I once said to Steve that I'd like to give him the details of how well he did last year. "Tell me in five years," he said. It's an attitude of mind. They're doing the work and they assume that I'm doing the business. All they want to know is where and when they've got to work.'

It is a system based on total trust of Hearn. 'Steve and I have always got on well because we trust the other's doing his job. I look after off the table and he looks after on the table. The rules are the same. We both play hard and we both play to win, and the day we don't we'll get sloppy and get beat. How we operate is based on how we got where we have got, by working hard and being competitive.'

Competition drives Hearn. It explains why he did not retire on his winnings from Riley Leisure, and why, at close to his fortieth birthday, he runs in marathons as a hobby. It began in 1981 after he had given up smoking. His weight rose from 12 stone 7 pounds to 15 stone. One day he ran for the train at Romford station and was still panting when it got to Ilford, four stops down the line.

He took up running, and it became as addictive as the nicotine had, and then there had to be targets, to run a marathon, to run one in three and a half hours, in three and a quarter, in under three. So far his best is three hours twenty-two minutes. 'Sometimes I think when I'm out running on a freezing cold morning, I'm worth a few quid, what the hell am I doing this for, why not stop off for a drink or a massage? It's the easy option, isn't it? You have to have targets in life, or you slip away and start boozing or birding and the like.'

His worst experience was in New York in 1987. He had had a busy month, co-promoting the heavyweight boxing match between Frank Bruno and Joe Bugner, and on an unusually warm November day his feet blistered, forcing him into a first aid station. Lying on the next stretcher was an older man, his leg muscles twisted as though a washerwoman had rung them out. 'You going on?' asked a paramedic attending him. 'Of course,' said the man. 'How about you?' he asked, turning to Hearn. 'Now what could I say?' He finished but it took him four hours fifteen minutes. 'It became a challenge to finish,' he says.

All his team are competitive. Hearn laughs at suggestions of fixes in snooker, of his eight deciding results. They are so competitive that when they had to decide how to share out the profits from Matchroom's endorsements at the end of the year, they decided to put on their own tournament and play for the money.

Each player was paid his daily rate for any work he had done promoting the endorsements or representing Matchroom's sponsors but the £125,000 remaining was put up as prize money at their own tournament in Southend. Willie Thorn, the £2,000 a day man, beat Steve Davis, the £5,000 a day man, in the final to take the £50,000 first prize. 'I used to play God and decide, which was OK when there was only shillings involved,' says Hearn. 'Now the fairest way is for sportsmen to play sport for the money. And charging people to watch them do it is a nice bonus. The players are a co-operative, but one based on winning. It's not equal share for all, but the most to the best.'

In the snooker world, the players pay their own way. Prize money is high but so are travelling and accommodation expenses. Griffiths reckons he covers so many miles that he must replace his BMW every six months. Davis has a Porsche but most often uses what is called 'the firm's car'; the 'Matchroom Bluesmobile', a 'dirty, great Cadillac', as Hearn describes it, which has a video, television and fridge in the back and is driven by Robbo Brazier, a long-time friend of Davis and Hearn.

A player who has turned down exhibition and appearances for a week to play a tournament will be losing out if he goes out in an early round. Hearn reckons that to make tournament play pay, one of his eight must reach the quarter-finals every time. 'Steve makes £5,000 a day, so in the fourteen days of a big tournament he could make £70,000. Only in the world championships could he win more than that and if he gets knocked out earlier he is losing badly. He has to win just to finish a little way down. If he goes out early we could rightly say that he hasn't won three and a half thousand, say, but lost fifty grand.'

Tournaments happen to be the part Davis enjoys. The major tournaments are also those where the other players can make their reputation and raise their market price. And among those in the Matchroom team who may be earning £150,000 a year that is a serious concern. Hearn reckons that a player must earn at least £100,000 to get a reasonable living from the game. 'After I've taken my twenty per cent and he's paid his travelling, accommodation and all the other expenses of his business, he'd come out with between thirty and forty thousand, and that's hardly riches. And nothing's forever. They only have to look at Kirk Stevens to know that.'

Stevens was a world-class player, popular and with talent, whose form deserted him after he admitted taking drugs. He sank down the world rankings. 'My eight happen to be some of the world's top players now but in two years how do they know where they will be? They get paid for success and only as long as they are successful, and I wouldn't begrudge them a penny of it.'

The money goes to Hearn who takes his twenty per cent and then puts it in the player's own limited company which, technically, employs him. At the end of each month the player gets a salary cheque, and sometimes a bonus if he has a special need that month. Davis' salary is paid annually, largely because he spends so little. His only extravagance since he bought a working farm in Essex where he lives with his mother and father is buying soul and jazz records. On the road, the players pay their way with credit cards which their company settles. 'I only need cash for tips,' says Davis.

Hearn has created twenty-one companies around Matchroom. 'Or is it twenty now? I can never remember.' He is not a shareholder of any player's company but he has a partnership with Davis in an investment company which owns properties in London and a forest in Scotland. Most of Davis' earnings go directly into investments. But it is the Matchroom company itself, still based in The Arcade in Romford and still private ('independence is too valuable to go public'), which controls the operation.

In the last two years it has set the pace for the game itself, going its own way to the point where Hearn felt obliged to resign from the World Professional Billiards and Snooker Association board when Matchroom decided to promote rival tournaments abroad as part of a World Series. To Hearn's mind, snooker has become too dependent on television and too dependent on Britain, just as show jumping did before it took a dive in the popularity stakes. 'If snooker ever goes the way of horse jumping, I will only have myself to blame,' he says.

Matchroom set about putting that right by creating their own league, consisting of their own seven players and Canada's world number two Cliff Thorburn who has since joined Matchroom. It played at fourteen locations around Britain for a total prize fund of £75,000 with television barred. Even so, sponsors Rothmans agreed to put up sizable funds for the first two years with the hope that in the second year the league would reach into Holland, West Germany, Spain and Belgium.

Hearn realizes that snooker must seek wider audiences, and those lie abroad in countries where green baizes mean the game of pool and 'Minnesota Fats' playing 'Fast Eddie'. When snooker took off in Britain, the game was a strictly 'Empire' affair. Only in Canada, South Africa and Australia were there other professional players. It was Matchroom that played missionary to take the message to a wider world.

It began in 1982 when Hearn received an invitation from the editor of the *Bangkok Post* in Thailand to bring Davis and Meo there to play exhibitions and games against local amateurs. There he was introduced to the general who ran the Armed Forces television station and some games were screened. Each year Hearn was invited back, eventually adding Hong Kong, Malaysia and Singapore to the trip.

Subsequently, Matchroom took the game to Brazil, China and Hong Kong, and Hearn realized that here was the chance for a game to sell itself to the world. At the end of 1986 Matchroom decided to launch a World Series, a collection of tournaments in different countries in which players gained points towards an overall title. Their players would take part, but more important Matchroom would co-sponsor with the sports marketing company CSS. Ironically, the tournament in Hong Kong was sponsored by Riley Leisure. British-Caledonian Airways sponsored in Japan and brewers Labatt in Toronto. 'The biggest gamble of my life,' Hearn called it when he announced the launch.

It is a gamble because Hearn and Matchroom have gone into it as venture capitalists. The players are guaranteed prize money but if the Series loses money – and the tournament in Hong Kong did – it will be they and Hearn who will be the losers. 'I've never been one to take guarantees,' says Hearn. 'I gamble on success.' The early signs were that he had backed another winner. The tournament in Toronto had fourteen hours of television, including three hours live for the final in CBC's peak hours.

Hearn sees event promotion as his own future. Co-promoting the fight between Bugner and Bruno with Bruno's manager Terry Lawless and Mickey Duff was another step towards it. 'Promoting an event is much easier than managing another player. That's not easy. They are all individuals, all different. Just because you have managed Steve Davis doesn't make it easier managing Neal Foulds. Everyone is a new experience. You have to talk to them differently, address their problems differently, advise them differently. You are handling human emotions and they are always different.

'Promoting a sports event is easier. There's no problem you can't solve because if one's too big you walk away and try something else. It's just a bit of business. You ask a sportsman to do a specified job for you. In a sense you employ him for a period to make money for you. You know how much you are giving him and he knows what he has to do in return. You make your arrangements, sit back and enjoy the spectacle. When the event is over, that's it, profit or loss. You're not worrying about the follow-ups, the after-effects, players wanting to cry on your shoulder.'

It is not that easy, or everybody would be doing it. Hearn spoke of such ease before the Bugner–Bruno fight and after his first experience of boxing promotion at Southend where there were just 900 spectators and no television. Steve Davis came along and so did Hearn's eight-year-old son and fellow director, Edward. 'Told Mickey Duff to get out of his seat, he did,' says Hearn with a laugh. 'We had a lot of fun and we spent the profit on a Chinese meal on the way home,' he says.

Bugner–Bruno, the sequel, was not so easy. 'I'm used to pressure but never pressure like that,' he admits. 'I didn't enjoy it like I do usually. It wasn't that there was any risk on the money. It was covered or insured, and because almost everybody was on a percentage there were no great deductions to worry you. It was just being out there exposed, everybody knocking the fight and saying what a joke it was. Fortunately, it was a long way from being the worst fight ever, and everybody had a good night, but I was scared hairless that people wouldn't think they had had value for money. I mean, what would have happened if Bugner hadn't got past round one?'

Hearn had known Lawless as a friend and neighbour for years, and proposed the fight when the Canadian Trevor Berbick pulled out of a scheduled fight with Bruno. 'I was there within seconds with my offer,' says Hearn. 'Terry didn't really want the fight for Bruno but with a fight that could make such a lot of money what choice did he have?'

By coincidence, the *Sunday Mirror* floated the idea of Bugner – Bruno the next morning but Hearn was a month ahead of them. He had spoken already with Tottenham Hotspur Football Club's chairman Irving Scholar about a date and done a deal for use of the ground – Spurs to get a percentage of the gate and all the ancillaries, like catering. His sums had been done before Berbick had hurt his back.

Bruno himself was offered 35 per cent which Lawless accepted as better than a straight fee. Bugner was on a fee of £250,000, plus the cost of sorting out his legal problems when he returned to Britain ('about £14,000') and the Australian television rights. 'If a boxer doesn't make from a percentage it is because he hasn't drawn a crowd. It's down to him. Either he is a client and gets paid a fee, or he wants to be part of the action in which case he takes part of the risk. Bugner took the fee and never moaned when Bruno who took the risk ended up with much more. I'm paranoid about people thinking they have been cheated but they can't have a guarantee and a percentage. None of us are in the insurance business.'

Bruno made more than his opponent because ITV bought the rights for a delayed transmission just one hour after the fight. ('Added a nought, that did, compared with next day transmission,' says Hearn.) And nearly 30,000 paid prices up to £100 to watch. There were also little touches that Hearn brought to the business, like a number you could call up on British Telecom and hear Bugner and Bruno talking. 'They had 50,000 calls. Small beer but it could be big one day.'

Hearn found the difference between boxing and snooker hard to fathom. A boxer on the bill at his show at Southend was lucky to get one-quarter of what Denis Taylor gets for an after-dinner speech. 'And he isn't getting the hell knocked out of him.' Yet the boxing spectator will pay far more than the snooker fan. The cheapest seat at Southend was £15, ringside seats were £30 and there were no famous names on the bill. Hearn would not expect to charge more than £10 for a seat to watch Davis play White, the two best players in the world.

The problem for snooker, as Hearn sees it, is that it has become too dependent on television. It is why Matchroom have promoted their League with sponsorship from Rothmans in which the top players meet in venues slightly bigger than the traditional halls and without television.

Major boxing, too, has made itself dependent but Hearn does not believe that there is any need. It is far better equipped than snooker to achieve success without the crutch of TV because it can have a large enough live gate paying high enough prices to support it. He has looked at most of the available big halls as potential venues and earmarked some still being built. 'In fact, if you had live television it would deter spectators and probably cost you more in gate receipts than you make from the TV fee. Television should only be for mega-shows which will sell out anyway. I'm sure that there is business, for the fighters and promoters, in small non-televised shows.'

In his first year in the fight game Barry Hearn has worked with Terry Lawless. He has taken on Terry's son Steve at Matchroom to help out on the boxing side but it is Hearn who has stood to win or lose. He found that what he had learned as a manager was invaluable as a promoter. 'The two overlap in so many areas, and particularly television which is an area every manager must be on top of these days.'

Quite what makes Barry Hearn run, he isn't sure. Not money certainly. He has an impressive old country house in Essex, with a housekeeper and handyman and private gymnasium; and he is content with his Jaguar car. 'Bugner–Bruno wasn't about money. I didn't give a monkey for it. It was a challenge, something people had talked about but said wouldn't happen. Money's just the sidebar. It's in my nature to make a deal which will make money because if not I wouldn't feel I was playing the game. Me not making money from a promotion is like the fighters not training for a fight. It would be unprofessional. But it's not the reason for doing it.

'I suppose in the end I do it because that's what I enjoy doing. I don't take days off because I don't consider what I do is work.

To make a living out of sport is unbelievable. My mother can't believe I do. I enjoy every day, and I look forward to the next. Please God it lasts for ever.'

The football fan who bought a club – Irving Scholar, the chairman of the Tottenham Hotspur Football Club in North London.

6

THE CLUB

THERE must be many people who have dreamed of owning their own football club, who have envied the men with the best seats in the ground, a scotch at half-time in the board-room and the right to be addressed as 'Mr' by the star player. And which football supporter has not thought that he could make a better job of running a club?

Directors are a curious breed: local butchers, bakers and candlestick makers who find a curious thrill in an association more likely to earn them the contempt of their neighbours than their gratitude. Few have played the game and fewer understand it. 'The ideal board of directors should be made up of three men – two dead and the other dying,' suggested the manager and former international player, Tommy Docherty.

It is a sentiment close to the hearts of most of the game's professionals. There is little love lost on the men who guarantee the loans that pay their wages. 'Soccer is run by second-rate con-men,' suggested Eamonn Dunphy, an international footballer who turned in retirement to writing. 'Petit-bourgeois, frustrated, small businessmen.' Another international player, Len Shackleton, dismissed their claim to any importance by leaving a chapter of his autobiography headed 'Directors' entirely blank.

It is a mute point then whether soccer could have survived without directors or would have succeeded better without them. Since directors run every professional club in Britain, form the management committee of the Football and Scottish Leagues and, to a large extent, dominate the ruling bodies of their Football Associations, they are as responsible for all that is wrong with the game as they are for the money which has kept it in business.

Being a director of a football club in England is unlike any similar company appointment. For the first 100 years of the League, the rules of the Football Association expressly forbade directors from receiving payment. Dividends were limited by League statute and were extremely rare because few clubs made profits. Even today only one director may be paid. The others, by tradition, are still expected to dip into their pockets to pay the bills or at least guarantee the loans from the banks.

In 1982, the year the FA first allowed paid directors and not an exceptionally bad season for English football, Wolverhampton Wanderers, once the grandest club in the country, admitted debts of £2.5 million. Birmingham City of the First Division confessed to owing £1.2 million, Rotherham £1 million and Bristol City to having run up a £700,000 deficit by losing £4,000 each week.

Only nine of the ninety-two clubs in the Football League were said to have made a profit on the previous season. Newcastle United lost £877,381, Arsenal almost £500,000, Manchester United, whose matches were the best attended, still managed to lose money and Sir Arthur South, chairman of Norwich City predicted that hundreds of players would be on the dole at the end of the season after his club reported a loss of £327,000.

It was soccer's age of the profligate. The price of players – and their rewards – soared to unprecedented heights while the number of spectators fell by another million. Average attendances at matches were the lowest ever recorded while clubs completed grandiose plans to build new stands. Charlton Athletic, with attendances averaging only a tenth of their 1938 record attendance, opened a new stand – and three years later were forced to leave their ground – and Chelsea admitted that the cost of their new stand had crippled them. Wolves' financial problems had also started with the re-development of their Molineux ground and Nottingham Forest, a club traditionally run by a committee, had been forced into becoming a private limited company by the building of their new ground.

Tottenham Hotspur Football Club, or Spurs to the football fan, were more successful than most clubs at the time. Their average attendance the previous season of 35,099 had been exceeded only by Manchester United. In the previous two years, they had won the FA Cup twice, lost in the Milk Cup final and reached the semi-final of the European Cup-Winners Cup. In eighteen months they had played at Wembley Stadium seven times, setting a British record for receipts of £918,000 when they met Queen's Park Rangers there in the 1982 FA Cup final.

The club was also £5.25 million in debt, the greatest burden of debt ever suffered by a British football club and dwarfing those which were said to be crippling its West London rivals Chelsea. Again the fault lay with a decision of a board of directors to invest in a new stand; a stand which Spurs needed but which they could finance only by massive borrowing.

Since the public announcement of the building of a new west grandstand in 1979, Irving Scholar had feared that it would be beyond the club's resources. He can still remember the day when the *London Standard* broke the news on their back page with an artist's impression of the new building, and a friend phoning him at his office. 'See the *Standard*,' he said. 'They are going to get themselves into trouble with this one.'

It was Scholar's own feeling. The story in the *Standard* reported a cost of £3.5 million, but looking at the drawing Scholar thought that conservative. He was a commercial and industrial developer and knew that costs invariably over-shot the target. He thought it would cost closer to £5 million, and the cost of borrowing so much would make it impossible for the club to compete for the players they needed.

Soccer has always been in an invidious taxable position. What it receives from the sale of players to other clubs is income, and a profit spent on another player can be written off. A profit spent on ground improvements is capital expenditure and incurs Corporation Tax (then at 52 per cent). 'To a businessman it was obvious why so many clubs were getting themselves into trouble over ground improvements,' says Scholar.

There was opposition to the way it was proposed that the new stand would be financed within the Spurs board. Sydney Wale, the chairman who was the biggest single shareholder with fourteen per cent, had resigned the chair over the issue. To Scholar, the outsider, it mattered only because he was a supporter.

The club was his recreation ('my only true love'), and had been since he was five years old and an uncle took him to a match at White Hart Lane. 'I couldn't sit still I was so excited.' He lived in Hendon, an area more in the catchment area of Spurs' arch rivals Arsenal, but it had been love at first sight.

By the age of twelve he was travelling to away matches, unbeknown to his parents who were told that he was visiting friends. Those were the days when Spurs were becoming the first club this century to win Cup and League in the same season, grounds were often full, and Scholar on at least one occasion climbed a gate when the turnstiles were closed. 'My parents found out eventually and were waiting in the car park when I got back from a game in the Midlands. They didn't stop me, only made sure after that that they knew the trains I would be catching and when I'd be home.'

Scholar had graduated by the end of the sixties to the status of season ticket holder at White Hart Lane. He had begun work as an estate agent, dealing with commercial properties, and a string of coincidences had led him into a prosperous property business. 'I became friends with Keith Wickenden who was a partner in a large firm of accountants and whose brother was the chairman of a public company, Townsend Thorenson. When the brother died, the company invited him to become chairman and he moved the operation into the same building my company occupied, so we became closer friends.'

The two men formed a joint company called Townsend Thorenson Properties which became European Ferries' property division later. 'He was very much my mentor, a man who backed people he liked and trusted and he backed me.' They had one other thing in common. Wickenden was keen on football and was to become vice-chairman of Brighton and Hove Albion FC before his own death in a plane crash.

But Scholar's own involvement then with Spurs was strictly as a supporter. He was on nodding terms with the more established players, like Steve Perryman and Glenn Hoddle, because he had been travelling away with the supporters' group on trains and planes for so long, but he knew nobody in authority. Still, the stand project had interested him as a developer and supporter.

Initially he did nothing more than attend a meeting called by the club in an attempt to pre-sell the seventy-two executive boxes they planned in the new stand. They were asking £30,000 as three years rent in advance and managed to sell twenty-eight of them. That inspired him to write to the club chairman, Arthur Richardson, telling him of his background in property and warning him of the likelihood of over-shooting the budget. The club were not interested in his help, and for another year he remained in the background, doing no more than make a few enquiries about the club's constitution.

What he found intrigued him. Spurs had become a limited company in 1898, three years after it had started paying players and ten years before it was elected to the Football League. The club's directors had offered 8,000 £1 shares for sale but although they left the issue open until 1905, it closed with only 4,892 sold. That was how many were still held in 1982.

There was good reason why clubs kept the shareholding small. Most became private fiefdoms and in turn family dynasties. The Cobbolds controlled Ipswich, the Mears Chelsea, Hill-Wood Arsenal and the Cearns West Ham. Issuing shares meant them investing more money or relinquishing some of their power, and directors had preferred the alternative of allowing the club to subsist on its trading profits and borrowing. Those who got into trouble did so because they had not raised enough capital.

Scholar found another idiosyncracy. In the 1920s the Spurs directors had tried to stop a person they disapproved of becoming a shareholder. They took the case to court and lost but at a subsequent annual meeting had passed a new article of association which gave the right of directors to refuse to recognize the transfer of a share without their consent. It was Article 14 and it empowered them to refuse recognition without giving any reason.

It was tested in court in 1936 by a Mr Berry, a constant critic of the board of directors of the time. This time the Spurs directors won in a case which became an often-cited precedent in English law. So the Spurs board had the right of veto not only against newcomers joining the board but also against anyone buying as much as a single share. They were a self-perpetuating oligarchy.

In December 1981, still concerned at the club's financial

prospects and encouraged in his concern by other supporters, Scholar went to a shareholders meeting armed with the proxy vote of a friend. When he tried to ask a question, Richardson the chairman, declined to listen. Scholar protested, the club's legal adviser intervened to support his right and the club at least had to answer. 'All I wanted to ask was about the costs of the stand and the answers I was given were not the answers I though I should be getting,' he says.

At that point Scholar decided he would buy the club, and he had support. Paul Bobroff, chairman and managing director of Markheath Securities, a listed public company, was another season ticket holder who sat a row behind Scholar and was as concerned. 'We sensed that they were going to the edge of the precipice and nobody was prepared to do anything,' says Scholar. Within a month, they had laid plans for an ambush.

It was a clever plot. Scholar ascertained from the register of shareholders that there were many women among them, the widows and daughters of men more interested in the game. One, curiously, was the widow of Mr Berry, the club's thirties critic. Scholar calculated that they were less likely to have any emotional attachment to their shares and wrote to them first.

'Instead of asking each of them if they wanted to sell, I made a direct offer for each of their shares. It seemed so much more definite than just making inquiries whether they would sell,' he says. 'I thought it was more likely to get their attention.'

The difficulty was in valuing the shares since so few transactions ever took place. 'I didn't want to spend too much money on shareholders because I preferred to spend it eventually on the club. I worked out what I could afford and how many shares I needed for control, and then did my sums.'

The board itself controlled only 400 shares because of the split with Wale but it was possible that they would be able to round up more support from the old faithfuls among supporters. So Scholar and Bobroff settled on a target of a full controlling interest.

The response was immediate and enthusiastic. Women wrote asking when he would send a cheque. Most had no interest in the club and would have sold sooner had anybody approached them. Those who asked why Scholar was buying were told that he was a fan. 'Not untrue but I could not divulge everything about my motives,' he admits. When he wrote to Mrs Berry, after tracking her to the Midlands, he felt confident enough of her husband's anti-establishment stance to tell her his motives. 'She was delighted, and said her husband would be smiling in his grave,' says Scholar who was encouraged to part with a cheque of £34,000 for her 136 shares.

Over nine months he wrote 300 letters, while Bobroff bought his share in one large block, namely the family holding of the late F.J. Bearman who had been a director for fifty years and chairman when the club won the double in 1960 – 61.

Because their lawyers advised them that Article 14 still applied, they transferred none of the shares to their own names but asked the owners to give them their proxies. The two reached a controlling 50 per cent without a single change showing on the shareholders' register, and then presented the board with their fait accompli. The two Richardsons resigned along with one other director while two other directors, Douglas Alexiou and Frank Sinclair, were invited to remain. The first decision of the new board was to remove Article 14. And when it was done, Scholar admits he felt like the boy who had been given the key to the toy factory. 'I think you could safely speculate that there was a smile on my face,' he says.

The secrecy of their blind-side run on the Spurs camp had posed one more problem for them. It is normal in a take-over to have a detailed investigation of a company's books but because of the certainty that their bid would be contested – which it was once it became common knowledge – Scholar and Bobroff's accountants only got their hands on the books after they gained control officially in December, 1982. 'We had had a rough idea but we were rounding off numbers and it was worse than we expected,' says Scholar.

The debt could have been calamitous. 'They had been to Wembley seven times in eighteen months but they would have needed to win the FA Cup for the next ten years to pay it off,' says Scholar. 'We were in a far graver position than Chelsea and there had been headlines for months about them having to leave Stamford Bridge. Our team did not even have a sponsor for their shirts.'

The debt with the club's bankers was so large that no cheque could be signed over an agreed amount without consulting them. When the manager Keigh Burkinshaw told the new directors that he wanted to buy a new player two directors had to personally guarantee the further loan at the bank. 'Looking back, in the club's books it was obvious that things had never been that bad,' says Scholar.

The new board were, at least, happy with the running of the football side of the club. They had no complaints with the management of Burkinshaw although Spurs were beaten in the fifth rounds of both FA and League Cups, the second round of the European Cup-Winners Cup and finished fourth in the First Division. 'What was obvious was that unless something was done quickly about the debt, we would be in the position of having to sell players, and for a supporter like me that was an untenable position,' he says.

That day was postponed temporarily the following summer by a rights issue to existing shareholders which raised £1,350,000, and took Bobroff and Scholar to a position of holding more than 90 per cent of the club. Under section 209 of the Finance Act they became automatically the owners of 100 per cent. Their next move was to make Tottenham Hotspur Football and Athletic Club Limited unique in British football as its first public company with a Stock Exchange listing.

'The club had a phenomenal record on the field which was producing high receipts but it was among the walking wounded because of the debt,' said Scholar. 'It was obvious to us that it could be a profitable business if the debt could be stripped out. So why not go public? Every type of company under the sun had a listing, and leisure shares were doing well. Why not a soccer club?'

Why not, indeed? Just because no club had done it did not mean that it could not be done. So why had none tried it? All needed capital, and would have been better able to expand their operations with it. So where was the catch?

The first was easily disposed of. Football League regulations limit dividends to shareholders and, in the event of winding-up, dictate that assets go to shareholders 'at par' while the rest goes to the Football League. That was not feasible for a public company but it was surmounted by making the club only a subsidiary of a holding company which would be the public company and take all the profits. Scholar became chairman of the club and Bobroff of the limited company.

'We kept waiting for somebody to tell us we couldn't do it, the League or the FA or somebody, but nobody did. It just seemed that nobody had ever wanted to, so nobody had ever tested the rules.'

Tottenham Hotspur plc went to the market in 1983, with Scholar holding 2,659,000 shares (29%) Bobroff 1,441,800, (15.7%) and the three other directors just 1 per cent, and was offered to the public at 3,800,000 25p shares at 100p each. The issue was four and a half times over-subscribed, and Scholar, Bobroff, Alexiou and Sinclair retained slightly more than 50 per cent between them. The club's debts at the time of the issue of £3,287,952 were wiped out.

At the start there were more than 14,000 shareholders with an average shareholding of less than 300 shares. Among them were many fans and even a few soccer writers. They were not going to get rich quick. After the opening day on the Stock Exchange the shares did not return to 100p for three years, at one time dropping as low as 64p, but the fans wanted only to feel part of the club and the institutions were looking on the investment as a long-term prospect. 'More and more over the first three years, we have had institutions buying in,' says Scholar.

Scholar has found some disadvantages in being part of a public company. 'We are under the microscope more than the ordinary board of directors. For one thing we have had between 400 and 600 people turn up at our annual meetings. We also have a greater responsibility than the boards of other clubs and are obviously far more publicly accountable. But none of those are bad things and the advantages are obvious.'

In the first year of the Scholar – Bobroff regime Spurs posted a profit of £900,000 after winning the UEFA Cup, and the second year a profit of £600,000. The first loss came in the season after the Heysel Stadium disaster when all English clubs were banned from European competition and domestic attendances went down. Spurs slumped to an average gate of only 21,000 and the club lost £662,000; the company not bothering to pay a dividend. 'The public lost confidence in football, not Spurs in particular,' says Scholar. Fortunately, it did not last. Spurs attendance leapt 24 per cent and the profit for the year until the end of May 1987 was £971,000 and a final dividend of 4p was paid.

'It's often said that when businessmen go into football they leave their commercial acumen behind,' admits Scholar, who keeps his hand in by continuing to run a property company but devotes most of his time – and interest – to Spurs. 'It's true to a point but there is one thing that makes the difference. When he runs his own company he makes the decisions and not too many people are interested. When he's running a soccer club, there's tens of thousands interested and he can be criticized in the newspapers every day. So it makes a businessman wary, perhaps over cautious, but most of all over indulgent which is what normally leads to the problems.

'But soccer's great problem is that those in authority do not employ good business principles. Perhaps they have forgotten them. Some in senior positions never knew any. There are too many managers who have no commercial experience, like the ex-players. One manager told me he had done a two year course in finance – one week one year, one week the next. And club directors do not enforce financial controls on them. A football club should be like any good company, with proper budgeting and forecasting for instance, Spurs try to get the transfer account balancing. We're flexible but we have to know where we're going. The manager has to be responsible for his department. I used to think when I was a kid reading about the game that all those £1 million transfers were toy town money. When you have to sign the cheques, you realize it's all very real.'

Scholar sees nothing incompatible in making his hobby pay, in spending so that his team win while ensuring that his company makes profits. 'The two are the same,' he argues. 'A winning team means a successful company, more people watching and more games played. You are investing in the team to get a return in profits. First you have to have the capital to invest. You can't only do it from borrowings. Going public is one way to get the capital.'

But business principles must be applied, whether it is sport or property. The problem of a football league club which is obvious to anybody is its dependence on a product which it can offer to its public only about twenty-five times each year in a ground which remains unused for at least 330 days in the year. So Spurs decided upon two courses – greater use of the ground for non-soccer events and diversification of the company into related fields.

Diversification was easier. Scholar had initially done a deal with the French sportswear company Le Coq Sportif as the club's kit suppliers and shirt sponsors. Each replica of the Spurs kit which the company sold produced a royalty for the club. Scholar thought more could be made of the equipment deal, and when another straight royalty deal was offered by Hummel, a company large in its native Scandinavia but little known in Britain, he suggested that Spurs create and own Hummel UK Ltd to distribute their products in Britain.

Spurs opened a warehouse at Enfield, employed a former Adidas executive as its group marketing director and after only one year was realizing profits. 'Now we not only get a royalty on every Spurs shirt Hummel sell but a profit on everything else,' says Scholar.

Spurs were in the marketing business already. They had sold seasons's leases to seventy-two executive boxes in the new stand, most to major corporations like Barclays Bank, Rio Tinto Zinc and ICI, for an income of £850,000. 'They may look as if they are treated better than the average spectator but they are subsidizing other fans' entry prices,' says Scholar. It had its Spurs Shop adjacent to the ground, and a travel division which started to arrange the club and supporters travel and had expanded to cater for other business houses. It started a joint venture in conference and banqueting with caterers Letheby and Christopher and created a publishing division which published four books in its first year including one on Manchester United. 'You only have to look at how well the National Football League in America markets everything from balls to cut glass to realize the potential that English soccer has been ignoring. People published books about Spurs, sold products with the Spurs name on them, sold package tours to Spurs matches and the club never made anything from them. It's ours, why not profit by it?' The company even won the exclusive rights from the Football Association to market souvenirs in England's colours from 1988.

There are international markets to be exploited because the Football League itself puts out a television recording of league action every week which is shown in forty-one countries, and between November and March a league match is shown live on Saturday afternoons in Scandinavia. It was that which created Hummel's original interest in marketing Spurs playing kit. Already Spurs have published a history of the club in Europe on video. 'Football clubs are an Aladdin's cave but the riches inside are untapped,' argues Scholar. 'Too much is given away to outsiders. If more clubs were in public ownership they might be forced to look more closely at capitalizing their assets.'

One asset not exploited had been the exposure offered by players' shirts. Spurs sold the right to that to German brewers, Holstein, who remain their sponors five years later. Such deals can be worth as much as £500,000 for a season on top of £300,000 which a top club can earn from its kit contracts with suppliers such as Hummel and Adidas. 'I would think that between twenty and fifty per cent of any club's income now comes from sources other than traditional receipts at the turnstiles,' says Scholar. A First Division club such as Spurs also share fifty per cent of the £1.3 million which Barclays Bank pay each season to sponsor the League as a whole. 'It is not a significant sum for us, but the prestige of a big bank as the sport's sponsor enhances its image considerably.'

To mastermind the non-football side Bobroff and Scholar invited another wealthy Spurs fan, Tony Berry, to join the board in March 1987. Berry, the chairman and chief executive behind the spectacular growth of Blue Arrow plc, the employment agency which had recently eaten up Manpower, bought 400,000 shares at £1.10 to become a non-executive director of Tottenham plc, Hummel (UK) and the club.

The most valuable, and least used, asset of any football club is its ground, a huge expanse of real estate often situated in sought-after residential areas. Even outside the obvious grounds in London, many clubs such as Oxford, Watford, Luton, Brighton, Ipswich and Norwich would do well to capitalize on their major asset by moving to modern stadia built in green field sites with greater parking and better access. But so long as they stay, usually, as Scholar admits, for nostalgic reasons connected with the core of their support, what they have could be put to better use.

Spurs have ruled out selling their ground and moving, although they did dispose of the club's training ground in the prized residential area of Cheshunt in Hertfordshire for £4,678,000 at the end of 1986, not with any thought to asset stripping but precisely to capitalize on an under-used and expensive asset. The money realized allowed the company to go on the acquisition trail, buying the freehold of three shops which they lease now and setting up a 1988 take-over in the sportswear market which would push Hummel beyond the 500 retailing outlets it estab-lished in its first year.

Tottenham's ground – called colloquially White Hart Lane – it actually faces Tottenham High Road – was occupied first in 1898 before the age of the car. It has no car parking of its own, and there is no public parking within a quarter of a mile. But the potential of an arena licensed to hold 50,000 in a catchment area of millions is enormous still. 'It is laughable that a major sporting venue, which is the biggest ratepayer in the Borough of Haringey, is used no more than thirty times in a year,' says Scholar. 'We have the experience of handling crowds, the security, the hospitality boxes, and it's not being used.'

The first move in that direction was a famous success. For the first time in thirty years, White Hart Lane was the venue for a major box-ing promotion, a ring in the centre circle and 31,000 watching a heavyweight fight in which Frank Bruno beat Joe Bugner. It was co-promoter Barry Hearn's idea, rather than Scholar's initiative, but he agreed immediately, believing that in big events lay the future for his ground. It was a feather in their cap that they were chosen before Wembley and survived a counter-bid from the famous stadium.

Spurs were on a percentage of the gate receipts – which were more than four times what any soccer match had produced and would have been £2.6million with a full house – and all the ancillaries, like catering. The discovery that the turf could be protected so successfully that the groundsman could hardly detect that so many people had sat on his pitch, opens up all sorts of possibilities. 'Five pop concerts and one fight like that in a year and we'd make more money from the ground than we do from all our soccer,' says Scholar.

So far in three years the new owners have, through diversifi-cation, greatly reduced the company's dependence on the fortunes of its football team. Soccer was already less than sixty per cent of Tottenham Hotspur plc's business when Berry took over the non-football operations, and the likelihood was that by the end of the 1987–8 season, when Tottenham Hotspur's turnover would be exceeding £11 million, it would be barely half.

How far can England's other ninety-one clubs follow Spurs down the business road? Scholar says that going public is a choice open only to the larger clubs but doing better business is open to all. 'There is no great secret about running a successful business, and soccer has any number of people who have been successful in business elsewhere.' The obvious examples like publisher Robert Maxwell, who chairs Derby County and whose son chairs Oxford United, and Martin Edwards of Manchester United, whose family fortune was founded on meat, are both hands-on chairmen who do not regard their involvement as philanthropic or patronage. They run their clubs as they run their businesses.

'Soccer isn't all failure and disaster. Let's give it credit for thinking ahead with executive boxes. There are twenty-eight clubs now with those, and if you provide good facilities like them, companies will spend £15,000 a season to use them, as we've found. People must stop thinking of soccer as some cottage industry. There are 500,000 people watching it every week for the best part of nine months of the year. Clubs like Spurs, Liverpool, Arsenal and Manchester United all turn over more than £5 million a year just on soccer. It is a huge industry we're running.'

But Scholar and Bobroff, the soccer fans who bought a soccer club, are not forgetting the game, or their fellow spectators. Some of the money realized from the sale of Cheshunt will be spent on providing a far greater percentage of seating at the Spurs ground. 'Just because you become chairman doesn't mean you have to get out of touch,' says Scholar.

When the club reached the FA Cup Final at Wembley in 1987, there was the traditional over-subscription for the club's allocation of tickets. Alleged Spurs supporters appeared from everywhere. There were more allocations than the club's average gates.

It recalled for Scholar one of the most miserable moments of his childhood in 1962 when Spurs reached the final to play Burnley. A fourteen-year-old, he had been to every Cup game that season, home and away, and most league matches, but in a ballot for tickets he was not one of the lucky ones. 'I remember exactly that

I was in Brighton the day I heard and that I was devastated. Oh, sure I could watch it on the television but people who had been to fewer Spurs games than I had would be there, at Wembley. The disappointment always stayed with me,' he says.

'From the time I became chairman I vowed that if we ever got to Wembley that would never happen. The FA Cup final should be the supporters' day, the real supporters, and you can't imagine my joy when we did get to Wembley. All the members of Spurs – and there are 17,000 – got a ticket. All seventy-two executive boxes got their share and, for the first time, every one of our 7,000 seated season ticket holders got a seat. We took the lot. It was a pity we lost but having the whole family there was one of the milestones that made all we'd done worthwhile.'

The membership scheme is another scheme to help the real spectator. Spurs installed closed circuit security television before the government demanded it and spent £150,000 on policing each season, but the introduction of a membership scheme for part of the ground promises to help them make savings in that department while giving the regular Spurs fan more comfort. In its first season not one person was arrested in that section and, for the next season, police agreed to remove the security fencing there. Members will soon be rewarded with more seating in their section.

Scholar does not believe that every club is ripe for what has been done at Tottenham, and he does not think many business-men would be interested in the exercise. In late 1987, the Spurs share price was well above the offer price for the first time, and eventually reached a high of 258p before the Stock Market crash.

He does not think that, looking at soccer as a pure investment, any businessman would have chosen Spurs when he did, although in 1986 an American, Isadore Brown, bought 13.67% of Spurs equity in an unsuccessful attempt to get on the board. Spurs rejected his overtures because 'he had nothing to offer us' but they did send him the autographed ball he requested.

There were better investment prospects in 1982. 'Chelsea and Fulham were the obvious clubs sitting there on valuable land in West London. If all you wanted was to asset strip, the residential potential was fantastic. Fulham with its ground overlooking the Thames was ideal for a property development. You could have picked up Chelsea at the time for £1.2 million. Now the most conservative estimate of its value is £15 million.'

Scholar, whose background was commercial rather than residential development, would not have felt right about using a football club for development. 'It would have been against the grain for somebody who loves football,' he says. 'Anyway, the only club which interested me was Spurs. That was my allegiance. I could never understand people becoming a director of a club they don't support. I was Spurs through and through. How could I become a director of Arsenal or Chelsea? My heart wouldn't be in it.'

Scholar has kept his own company, but his heart and soul are with Spurs. He was living in Monte Carlo at one stage but he has given that up to be able to occupy the chairman's office at Spurs and at only forty is younger even than Terry Venables, the manager appointed from December 1987. 'It takes an enormous amount of my time. It is a business for me now, not a hobby. I am quite single-minded. If I'm interested in something I want to do it to the best of my ability. I want it to be time consuming. I'm totally dedicated to it.

'When you have followed a team since you were five years old, stood on the terraces and been a season ticket holder, to be chairman of it at Wembley is a lifetime dream. I don't take it lightly, it's a great honour.

'We are not building a team. We are building a club. Directors, players, managers, teams will all go but the club will be there. My part is making it stronger, more viable, fitter, better. It's not me who wants to be a success. That's not the motivation. I want to see Spurs as one of the leading clubs in Europe and I want to do it by running it as a successful business. It can be done, and I'm a lucky man to be in the position to try to do it.'

Mickey Duff (right) shares in the glory of Lloyd Honeyghan's successful defence of his world welterweight title with trainer Bobby Neill. Duff manages Honeyghan and has promoted his fights.

7

THE PROMOTER

IT MAY not be inappropriate that the offices of Mickey Duff, purveyor of pugilism, are in London's Wardour Street, a few strides from Shaftesbury Avenue and in the middle of Soho. Boxing has always been the sport closest to the entertainment business and Duff and his partner Mike Barrett were for years its Barnum and Bailey.

Had boxing not claimed him Duff would never have wanted for a living in this square mile of show business. Or in the garment industry, or any other where a man thinks on his feet and a quick profit can be turned. If Duff had not invented himself, Damon Runyon would have created him — a natural street trader, loud checks, heavy rings and a scar, all trans-Atlantic assurance and Cockney candour; a man as sharp as his suits.

Others in Wardour Street trade actors, film extras, models and what are known colloquially as 'live acts'. For forty years Duff has been dealing in boxers; matching them, managing them and, most lucratively, promoting their confrontations. If you want a fight, he can arrange it – anything from six two-minute rounds at your local baths to world championships at Caesar's Palace, Las Vegas. He has boxers in all shapes and sizes, their weight, worth and phone numbers filed in a memory as prodigious as some of the numbers he deals in.

Duff was a boxer once himself, although one fighter Mickey Duff would never have promoted was himself. 'I wouldn't have crossed the road to see one of my fights,' he says, an opinion, which coming from a man who has long been regarded as the finest judge of a boxer outside America, must be unchallengeable.

Too many exponents of the noble art end up broken men but Duff was too shrewd to stay long enough in the ring to be hurt. The scars he wears on his cheek and the broken nose were inflicted by a car and any pain he has suffered in the fight game has been strictly in the region of his pocket and never more than superficial.

Duff took only four years inside the ring to realize that his future lay not in his own fists but in those of others. It took only a few more years to become a contender for the title of the most successful matchmaker, manager, agent and promoter of those more skilled at the trade of professional pugilism, boxing so clever outside the ropes that, ultimately, he promoted the fight which made more money than any in the history of the sport in Britain – the heavyweight championship of the world between Frank Bruno, of Britain, and the champion, Tim Witherspoon, of the Unites States.

But that, as Duff says, was a long way down the road, after the best part of half a century of wheeling and dealing in what he described to a jury in a libel case in 1987 as the 'tight-knit world' of boxing. None know its streets and back alleys better now but Duff was not born into it, or even to the name he chose to use in it.

He was born Monik Prager, the son of a rabbi who abhorred violence. For his first eight years he lived in a ghetto in the town of Tarnova, near Cracow, until his father took the family out of Poland in 1938 in the face of the growing anti-Semitism in Central Europe. When the family arrived, like many such refugees, in the East End of London, the boy could not speak a word of the local language, neither English nor Cockney, something hardly imaginable today in a man with the natural wit of the native.

Boxing was not something his mother or father would have approved of, nor was it anything in which the boy himself had any inherent interest. It was his evacuation, along with the other children in the capital when the German bombing began, which provided him with his introduction to the Marquess of Queensberry's Rules.

The young Prager was sent to a Jewish hostel in the Midland

shoe-making town of Northampton. One other boy there had boxing gloves and took a particular delight in challenging others to fight. Prager was a casual observer but as the boxer began to run out of opponents, he was goaded into trying his luck with the gloves. 'I'd noticed that all he was doing was swinging. I reckoned that I had a longer reach and if I hit straight, I would hit him before he hit me.' It was his first successful judgement in the business, and he soon took over as the promoter of the contests in the wash-room.

His parents still nurtured high hopes for him in the more peace-loving role of rabbi, encouraging the thought in their boy by sending him to a private orthodox religious school in the north-east of England. It was not to be a line of work for which he showed any natural aptitude, and soon his parents were asked to remove him. It had not helped his prospects of emulating his father that he had 'arranged' fights between other boys.

Back in the East End, Prager joined a boy's club. Boxing was a popular pursuit in them, actively encouraged to channel youthful exuberence away from less legitimate pastimes available in any big city, and Prager had a talent for it. He knew his parents would not approve but his answer was to change his name and disguise his involvement. Mickey Duff was 'borrowed' from a character in a James Cagney movie he saw at the time. 'I just liked the ring about it,' he says. 'It sounded right for a boxer.'

In three years, Duff had 123 amateur bouts, mostly in boys' clubs. He reckons he won about sixty per cent of them. 'I wasn't brilliant but nor were the kids I was fighting.' But there must have been something there because when he was fifteen years and eight months old he decided to add four months to his age in order to apply for a professional licence.

He was fighting as a professional before the war ended and, as he was to show in later life, his timing was perfect. Boxing became a thriving business in the immediate post-war days. A public starved of entertainment crowded the small halls. Boxers were not paid well but there was plenty of work and it was regular. Some halls had shows twice weekly in winter, and the big promotions made big money. A British heavyweight championship fight between Jack London and Bruce Woodcock drew more than 40,000 to Tottenham Hotspur football ground.

Duff himself kept busy at less famous venues, fighting either as a bantam or welterweight, winning far more fights than he lost but never having the flair or the punching power that would have made him a crowd-puller. The most he ever earned for a fight was £65 when he took on Jackie Collins, the lightweight champion of Wales, on a bill at Newport. 'I thought I had confiscated all the money in the country,' he says, but the fee was unusually high only because he was a last-minute replacement. 'Jack Solomons, the promoter, was desperate,' says Duff, who was asked to take the contest only after fighting the previous evening at Brighton.

Duff's last fight was on November 8, 1948. Nothing significant in the date but it was his sixty-ninth fight. 'I thought it was a good number for a man to end up on,' he says, a toothy grin spreading a thousand lines across his face. 'I had realized by then that I was limited. I had talent but I lacked physical strength. I'd turned pro too young and fought too often, and I had never allowed myself to develop. I was tired all the time. It was obvious I was past my best.' He was nineteen years, ten months old.

For a while he went into a clothing factory earning £15 a week, but one day in Petticoat Lane he bumped into an old friend from his boys' club days, recently demobbed, who fancied his chances as a professional. He invited Duff, who had more up-to-date knowledge on the fight scene, to come with him to the people who were going to promote him and give an opinion on any opponents they suggested. It led to him advising the promoters, two brothers, on which fighters to match on their shows. 'It was all strictly unofficial. I didn't have a licence to matchmake but they offered me £10 a week plus ten per cent of a season's profits and it was better than working in a factory.'

Three months later, Duff applied to the Southern Area Council of the British Boxing Board of Control for a matchmaker's licence. They were amused, at least. By tradition, matchmakers, the men who put together the fights on a promoter's bill, were older men, former trainers or managers who had been around long enough to be wise in the ways of the business. Duff was twenty. 'But I knew a lot of people, a lot of fighters and managers. I'd fought on the same shows, hung around the gyms and the changing rooms.'

The Council chairman, Victor Berliner, knew Duff was match-making unofficially for the brothers. He could see no harm in making the arrangement official but he persuaded his fellow members only by offering Duff his licence on one year's probation. Duff was the youngest matchmaker in Britain, possibly the world.

He was also one of the busiest. Eventually he was making matches for different promoters at shows throughout London and the south-east; little places mainly, like Shoreditch Town Hall and the Majestic Ballroom, Finsbury Park. He worked on a gate percentage rather than a fee, to keep him sharply aware of the market. 'A good match is only a good match if it is good at the price,' he says, a philosophy which has stood him in good stead to this day. He would organize a show at least weekly and on one occasion two on the same evening, but it was not easy money.

He branched out into management, handling the affairs of a Canadian, Solly Cantor, for a time, but, like the rest of boxing and most professional sport at the time, he was waging a losing battle against the government's Entertainment Tax which levied a percentage on every seat sold. 'Halls closed down like there was an air-raid on,' he says.

So Duff went back into the clothing business, working in a factory making duffle coats and within a year opening his own. His only involvement with boxing was acting as a cornerman, applying the sponge and swabs for heavyweight Peter Waterman at his fights. He came back only when the Entertainment Tax was abolished in the 1957 budget. 'I can remember sitting in my barber's chair having a shave when I heard the news,' he says.

That same year, with his friend Harry Grossmith promoting, he made a match between Terry Downes and Dick Tiger, another brilliant piece of timing. Both were to become world champions five years later, but Duff matched them for £195 in a memorable fight. 'One of the best I can remember,' he says.

A year later he was promoting for himself. Liverpool Stadium, once a centre of boxing, had fallen on hard times, like the city itself. When the promoter there died, Duff was invited by the BBBC's Central Area Council to take it over. Many thought it would be his downfall but instead, by bringing in local kids, he produced the crowds and turned a profit.

'My first promotion featured a kid calles Dave Rent. He was a local boy but he'd been fighting in the States for Rocky Marciano's manager, Al Weill. He'd run up sixteen wins out of eighteen when I brought him back and we sold out. I gave him a guarantee of $2,500 against twenty-five per cent of the gate, and he ended up with $6,000. Weill was so pleased he gave me a $100 note to put away for my kid Gary's barmitzva present. I put it in a savings bond and when he collected eventually it made him £400.'

Duff himself was making a living but not a fortune. His first 'office' had been a phone box at the end of the street and his filing system a little black book with every manager and fighter's phone number. On one occasion, when he left Gary in his pram outside the box while he made some calls, he went home without him. He had been on the phone so long he had forgotten his son was with him. 'When I got my first phone at home, my bills were £1,000 a year at a time many people weren't earning that much,' he says.

In his first ten years Duff was associated with more than 350 shows, either as promoter or matchmaker but he was never more than the third man in the boxing business. In Britain, in the sixties, boxing was Jolly Jack Solomons, complete with Churchillian cigar, versus Harry 'The Hoarse' Levene, gruff-voiced with a notable nose. It was a hate-hate relationship which went far deeper than any of the usual publicity stunts professional boxing indulges in.

Both, like Duff, were East Enders. Both had been unsuccessful fighters themselves and graduated through management into promotions. London-Woodcock at Tottenham was Solomons' first major success, and later he promoted Freddie Mills and Randolph Turpin, and even fighters Levene managed. The animosity began when the Boxing Board ruled that managers could also promote and Levene took out a licence, very soon threatening Solomons' promotional monopoly.

Duff was Levene's lieutenant. He was his matchmaker for big fight nights at Wembley and Manchester's Belle Vue and was to succeed to the empire only when first Solomons and then Levene retired. But he saw the dangers of the Board's rule change and opposed it. 'I had been a matchmaker first, then a manager, then gave up my manager's licence when the Board said you couldn't be both. Then I became a promoter but when they said promoters could also be managers, I argued that the promoters would end up with all the fighters. It was obvious, wasn't it? The fighters would all go to promoters because they could guarantee them the work.'

Duff held out for two years but it happened just as he had predicted. 'My rival promoters managed all the fighters I wanted on my shows and I couldn't get them to fight for me. So I had to go along and become a manager.'

It makes for complications. Duff promoted until recently with business associate Mike Barrett. Between them they decided which fighters they wanted to top the bill in their shows and negotiated with their managers. They agreed the shape of the rest of the bill and their matchmaker Paddy Byrne 'made the under-card' negotiating with the fighters' managers. One of them might have been Duff wearing his other hat.

'I don't find it awkward. You really can't be a manager today without being a promoter. You wouldn't be able to get your boys the fights they need. I had a bill which lost be £5,000 but I ran it as a promoter knowing that I'd lose at least £3,000 but willing to do it because some of my boys needed the fights. Promoters are the people in boxing who make the most but they are also the people who can lose the most. So many things can go wrong if you're not clever or even if you're unlucky.

'I promoted at Mile End Area. One summer I ran a weekly open air show. I got rained out nine Tuesdays in a row, and there were only sixteen in the season! Now that's just bad luck. Some people would go crazy if that happened. I've got the right mentality. It's the difference between wage-earners and businessmen. George Francis, who managed John Conteh, was a wage-earner. He had a fair idea of the value of fights and which fights to take for his men but he didn't like the responsibility. He preferred to be a trainer. And he's good at it. I know how to train a fighter but I don't have the stomach for it. Each to his own.'

Duff's own business is more complex because he has an 'arrangement' to share all profits with three others. Formerly it was his co-promoter Barrett, with whom he ran Duff–Barrett Promotions, businessman Jarvis Astaire, with whom he has also promoted and who has a major interest in Wembley Stadium, and Terry Lawless, who manages many successful fighters.

The arrangement was struck in 1978, originally because Lawless was managing many of the best fighters on the bills promoted by the other three but not making a fair return on his work. 'Terry's Terry,' explains Duff. 'He's a nice guy. He won't take money off fighters until they are getting well paid, say three or four thousand for a fight. That means he manages eighty per cent of them for nothing all the time and one hundred per cent of them for nothing until they are making money. The good fighters would come to him because he was generous. He didn't take anything off them, bought their equipment, put his hand in his pocket if they were hard up . . . he became Uncle Terry who looks after fighters.

'He'd have somebody like Maurice Hope who would win the junior middleweight championship of the world but didn't make any great money until then and retires after a couple of defences of his title; and all Terry had made for six years' work with him was £40,000. And while he'd been earning that forty grand, he'd had ten other fighters going through his hands who hadn't made it and had earned him nothing while we, who'd been promoting Hope, had made, say £200,000. It wasn't fair, and in the long run it wasn't going to pay us to keep it that way. When we made the arrangement he'd been in the game fifteen years and had no money.'

Duff denies that the arrangement was motivated by the creation of a 'cartel' which could dictate terms and monopolize the market. 'Terry was a friend, that's all.'

The profit-sharing arrangement demands that all put their earnings from boxing into a single kitty and divide it equally at the year's end. Lawless and Duff both put their manager's fees (twenty-five per cent of a boxer's earnings) into the pot, and Duff, Barrett (until he withdrew early in 1988) and Astaire contribute their promotional profits. 'It was all legal and didn't break any of the rules of the sport,' says Duff. When the safe at Duff's home was broken into and the document sold to a newspaper the Boxing Board cleared all four of any wrong-doing.

'The chairman said we had acted with good intentions but perhaps I should have realized how it would have looked if a person with bad intentions had signed such an agreement. I said "Mr Chairman, people with bad intentions don't sign agreements. Have you heard of two bank robbers signing agreements?"'

Which is just about where Duff came into the business of Bruno and Witherspoon. Lawless manages Bruno, the most promising British heavyweight since Henry Cooper, a block of a man, heavily muscled with a charming personality, which doesn't match his physique.

Gradually, and some said too slowly, Lawless had led him through a series of lesser or ageing opponents until he had a fair amount of experience and a record besmirched only by a single defeat by an American, Bonecrusher Smith. Even in that fight, he was considered unlucky, a victim of a single punch when he was leading heavily on points. 'He was so far ahead he could have declared,' in Duff's opinion. Still, it was a record that made him a potential opponent for almost any of the world's best heavyweights.

One such was Gerry Coetzee, who was ranked by the World Boxing Association as the number one challenger to their champion Tim Witherspoon. It was something of a problem for them. Coetzee was a white South African; Witherspoon was a black American. The WBA had been more lenient than most sporting federations in its attitude to links with South Africa but there was pressure on them in the United States to harden their stance. But how? They could not declare Coetzee a non-challenger without first removing South Africa from membership. At the same time no American promoter would stage a fight against him and the WBA could not force a black American to go to South Africa to fight him.

'They had a problem and I could see an opportunity,' says Duff frankly. The solution, he decided, was to remove Coetzee as number one challenger by the legitimate means of defeating him. He approached his associate Lawless. Would Bruno fight the white South African? Yes, said Lawless after consulting Bruno, but only if Coetzee denounced apartheid and disassociated himself from it.

Duff knew already that Coetzee was desperate for one last pay day. He was thirty already and the openings for a white South African past his best were few. Duff made a few enquiries and discovered that Coetzee had a black boy as a sparring partner who had been living in his house since he was thirteen and whom Coetzee had adopted unofficially. It was the angle he was looking for.

Coetzee agreed to say publicly that apartheid was appalling. He added that to stop black guys fighting white South Africans would be another form of apartheid, but Bruno and Lawless' honour was satisfied.

The WBA listened with interest to Duff's case for making the fight a final elimination to decide the next challenger to Witherspoon for the championship. 'It is logical,' said Duff. 'Bruno is ranked number five, Coetzee number one. If five beats one, he deserves to be regarded as number one, doesn't he?' The WBA, anxious to be rid of the South African problem, agreed, and Bruno, to everybody's relief, did the business by dispatching Coetzee inside the distance.

Witherspoon was a different proposition, a tough opponent for Bruno, strong and experienced. Duff would have preferred the Briton's chances against the Canadian Trevor Berbick, who held the rival World Boxing Council's version of the world title. Witherspoon, he calculated, could be beaten 'but it was not a result I would bet an arm and a leg on.' And Bruno's only real chance was to have the fight in England.

'The only good cause I could show for the champion to leave home to fight here was to show to Don King who had the rights to Witherspoon's next fight that he would make more money in Britain. In America Bruno and Witherspoon was nothing. Ceasar's Palace might have given $500,000, maximum. Witherspoon wasn't big in the States and Bruno was a nobody. In England I could guarantee we would do a million pounds, a million and a half dollars at the time. That was for the gate alone. That whetted his appetite.'

It is not uncommon for promoters, like King and Duff, to have an option on promoting a fighters next fight, even on occasions selling that option to another promoter at a profit, similar in its terms to the financial futures market. Duff, going into 1988, had a three-fight option on the Mexican world champion Jorge Vaca which he had demanded as part of the price of Vaca's successful bid for the title against Britain's Lloyd Honeyghan, a fighter Duff managed and promoted. Vaca gave up his independence in return for a challenge to the title while, for Duff, it was an insurance policy in the event of his own man losing the title, which, in the event, he did.

King himself became one of America's two most powerful promoters – the other, Bob Arum, who runs Top Rank Inc, is, by complete contrast, a Harvard law graduate who served on Robert Kennedy's staff when he was Attorney General – by cleverly playing the options game. He served four years on a manslaughter conviction after a rival in a numbers racket in Cleveland died, appearing on the boxing scene only in 1974: He was most noticeable because of a hairstyle which reminded one writer of 'a man who had just stepped out of his bath onto a bare electric wire'. He began by buying an option on world heavyweight champion George Foreman's next title defence, using money loaned by the Zaire government in return for a promise to stage the fight against Muhammed Ali in their capital of Kinshasa. By writing options into subsequent contracts he kept a grip on the world heavyweight championships.

That, beyond argument, is the richest prize in sport, as much for the fighter as the promoter. Larry Holmes made $6,625,000 after the deduction of his manager's commission when he held one version of the title in 1985. Michael Spinks earned a net $4 million after taking the title from Holmes. Mike Tyson, the current champion, earned $2.3 million in 1986, the year in which he won the combined WBA/WBC world title at the culmination of a series of heavyweight fights which King promoted with the admirable aim of producing a single world champion recognized by both governing bodies. Live gates (paying as much as $750 for a ringside seat) live world-wide television by satellite (pioneered by King for that Kinshasa fight) and closed circuit cinema links have, from the days of Ali, made the heavyweight champions of the world sport's richest men.

King had an option on Witherspoon, just as he had options on most of America's best heavyweights. Witherspoon, technically, was managed by King's son, Carl, but since Don King Productions owned the option on Witherspoon's services, it was with Don King that Duff negotiated. 'I never once spoke to Witherspoon's manager,' says Duff.

Duff, agreed Don King, could have Witherspoon as an opponent for Bruno at a venue in England on two conditions: Don King Productions co-promoted the fight and participated in profits, and it was staged at 1 am to suit peak-time programming on the east coast of America for the US cable television company HBO with whom King had a contract.

Duff has no idea to this day what King paid Witherspoon for the fight. Duff's deal with Don King Productions was 'to supply the services of Tim Witherspoon'. 'I only hope it was more than King declared here for the tax,' he said. (Witherspoon has since begun legal action against King over the events leading up to his subsequent defeat in a first round knock-out by Bonecrusher Smith.)

King, in turn, paid Duff a lump sum for 'supplying the services of Frank Bruno'. Duff gave that in total to Bruno, and agreed to pay him additionally a percentage of the gate receipts with a minimum figure guaranteed. In effect it was a share of the promotion's profits less Don King Productions' share. Duff will not reveal details but he says that Bruno ended up with more than the bottom-line guarantee.

It was a complex deal but basically it amounted to King paying one fighter, and putting a TV rights fee from HBO into the kitty, while Duff paid the other fighter and put into the pot any other television fees he could negotiate and the gate receipts. After the expenses of both sides, the profits would be split 50–50. 'Our only gamble was the gate. If it made only half a million pounds we would make no profit,' says Duff.

With that in mind, the major consideration was a venue. Duff had a contract with Wembley Stadium Ltd but their indoor arena was not large enough to produce receipts of more than £1 million. So he examined the possibility of using a football stadium. He had staged fights at the Arsenal and Queen's Park Rangers soccer grounds but never at the 92,000 capacity Wembley. 'We went there, put chairs round the centre circle, sat in the Royal box, worked out all the angles and eventually priced up the house, starting from £150 for a ringside seat.'

The fight was to draw 41,000 spectators, all seated, and earned £1.6 million on the gate, far more than the subsequent fight Bruno had with Joe Bugner at Tottenham's ground. That in turn did only fractionally better than Barry McQuigan's world title fight with Pedroza which had been staged similarly in the open air at the Queen's Park Rangers ground.

Duff argued at the time, and believes still, that there would have been more watching had British television not been allowed to screen the fight. After years of using television to make his promotions viable, Duff had become 'passionately' opposed to it. 'It'll be the ruination of boxing,' he argues now. 'There is going to be saturation, a few bad fights, viewing figures will drop and then TV will drop it like a ton of hot bricks. It happened in America, and it took years there for it to come back, and only then because casinos brought it back to attract gamblers. Gaming laws will prevent that in Britain. If it goes, it may never come back.'

But Duff's hands were tied on this occasion. He had a long-standing contract with the BBC that, if he used any of the arenas at Wembley, they could screen the fight. So he had to offer it to them. In turn King had sold his series of heavyweight fights to Britain's rival commercial channel, ITV, and they claimed the rights to the fight as part of the series. An impasse. Duff reacted angrily. 'I called it off, and refused to sign anything with King,' says Duff.

Eventually, after a suggested compromise by the BBC, a deal was done in which both TV companies could screen the fight. Duff did a deal for $600,000 with the BBC who split the fee with ITV. Duff refused live coverage, and the two tossed for first choice of delayed screening time. The BBC won but surprisingly chose the following evening to screen the fight. ITV settled for 9am on the same Sunday morning, and ran a commercial saying 'see it first on ITV'. When Duff objected that it was hitting the live gate, they changed it to 'Go to bed and see it when you wake up.' Duff believes that television cost him 10,000 spectators.

Television's wide coverge of the world's best fights has dealt a serious blow already, in Duff's opinion, to small shows in Britain. 'They've become a licnce to lose money,' he says. 'I don't do any more than I have to, and I have to do more than I'd like. Who can expect people to want to buy a ticket for second-class entertainment, go out in the cold, pay for parking, when they can watch better on their own tele. Football is suffering the same fate. We'll get people back into the boxing halls by keeping television out.'

Even so, the Bruno–Witherspoon promotion made a profit of around £850,000. The Duff side's take came to a little under £500,000 when they included Lawless's twenty-five per cent manager's commission on Bruno's share. It was, on paper, the biggest profit ever made on a boxing show in Britain. 'In real terms? Probably not. Henry Cooper against Ali at the Arsenal ground in 1966 did infinitely better. Wages now are, what, five times what they were then? We didn't make five times as much on Bruno – Witherspoon. Not three times as much. Bruno might have done a bit better than Cooper did but the £45,000 Henry got for that fight was big money for the time.' Bruno, like Cooper, lost.

Over the years Duff has done well for himself out of 'show-business with blood', as it was once described. He has managed three world champions and promoted dozens of world championship fights. He has come a long way since Mile End Arena, a converted bomb site behind Mile End tube station, and travelled far. In the seventies he was commuting the Atlantic so regularly that he flew a million miles in one year, and averaged for three years around 750,000 miles. It forced him eventually to move the centre of his operations to New York, and the flat he has kept in London is little more than a bed and phone. He has other, more comfortable homes in Los Angeles, New York and Tel Aviv, but denies he is a millionaire in British terms. 'I'm comfortable,' he says. 'I don't have to do what I don't want to do.'

It was more than he would have made of himself as a fighter. He remembers one memorable night as he left the ring after a win hearing a clatter behind him. Wonderful, he thought, nobbins, (the money thrown by a crowd as the traditional sign of their appreciation of a good fight). 'Nobbins, be damned,' shouted his trainer.'They're throwing half-bricks.'

Frank Williams, founder and inspiration of his own Formula I racing team, is confined to a wheelchair but has never become a passenger. 'I am still the Guv'nor,' he says.

8

THE TEAM

FEW THINGS in his life would please Frank Williams more than to see his racing cars line up on the starting grid for a Grand Prix attired in his racing livery. Not the yellows of ICI, or the red and white of Canon, or the white out of blue of Denim. Just the plain and simple dark blue of Frank Williams Racing Team, the original colours of the first Formula 1 car he put on the track in 1969 and which his friend, Piers Courage, drove to second place in Monaco and Watkins Glen that summer.

Those were the days when a motor-racing enthusiast like Williams could buy a car off the peg and put it on the track with an outlay of a few thousand pounds each season. With a few mechanics working for little more than love, free oil from Castrol and tyres courtesy of Dunlop, and, with the right driver and enough commitment, the car would be competitive.

Today it is a different business. Williams is still motivated by the same desire to go racing, like the kid of eighteen putting together a car in his father's garage, but for him the cost of being competitive has been magnified a million times. His weekend's sport demands the advanced technology of engineers and designers at the cutting edge of automotive research and development, a workforce of 110 at a purpose-built factory led by a brilliant designer, Patrick Head, and the vast resources to support them.

There is no profit in it for his company, and none of his teams creativity is ever patented. They work far beyond nine to five and

143

on most weekends and Bank Holidays, not to sell anything but to give two young men the best chance when they go racing. Success is measured by nothing more tangible than the place a car finishes in a Sunday afternoon race.

They do it because if they were not building magnificent machines to win Grands Prix for Williams they would be building bangers in their own back yards or racing them round Brands Hatch. They are enthusiasts like Williams. 'To work for me, three qualities are essential – a passion for racing, a love of work and a little imagination,' he says, not surprised that sixty such men turned out on New Year's Day in 1987 to keep his programme on schedule.

But for today's racing team, the enthusiasm of a few men is not enough. The fuel which keeps them on the road is money, bundles of it so large that only the wealthiest corporate entities can justify it to their boards and their shareholders.

Plastering his cars with the stickers of so many commercial sponsors that hardly any dark blue is visible is the price Williams pays to stay ahead of the race. And the benefactors those stickers represent are so important to the operation that Williams Grand Prix Engineering Ltd employ a man who does nothing but put them on their cars, a new sticker for every sponsor for each of the sixteen races.

Engines are the primary cost, a third of the team's budget. In the seventies there was one reliable engine, the Cosworth, and virtually every team used it. Its development had been funded by Ford and it could be bought off the peg and relatively cheaply. The advert of the turbo-charged engine changed that. Turbos are more sophisticated, demanding and expensive, and each team must develop its own.

When they pulled out of the sport in 1985, Renault estimated that it would have cost them between £60 and £80 million over four years to develop a new generation of engines; beyond their resources when the company had lost more than a £1 billion in 1984. Honda admitted that developing engines for Williams cost them more than five billion yen, which was then £21 million, and a third more if they helped a second team, as they did until 1987.

Then there is the shell of the car. A racing car's shell can cost £31,000, compared to £700 for a family saloon. Williams are so advanced in the development of carbon fibres and composites that they could take on aerospace work for the Ministry of Defence if they were not too busy contesting the world constructor's and driver's championships.

They have an autoclave for curing the carbon-fibre chassis of their cars, and up to eight cars are built during a season. They expect no change from £1 million for that process.

Every time they race, the two competition cars are brand new, having been totally stripped back to nothing; every part replaced, the inside refurbished, the outside resprayed and then rebuilt. Chassis number 4 still, but a whole new car. And there are sixteen Grand prix races every year.

To support the two racers there is an identical third car, which will be taken to races, and a fourth which may be taken to a circuit like Monaco where more is likely to go wrong in practice. Normally it would be used by the testing team, another drain on resources with its own transporter, mechanics and engineers, which uses the two drivers to test Head's innovations and improvements twenty to twenty-five times every year.

The drivers themselves do not come cheaply. The world champion, Nelson Piquet, might demand seventy-five per cent of all prize money (most drivers get only thirty per cent), all his travelling expenses and a huge retainer. It was $2.1 million when he joined Williams in 1985. Ayrton Senna, a Brazilian, is contracted to be paid $5.4 million by the Lotus team in 1988, and Piquet's latest retainer almost certainly tops $4 million.

Nigel Mansell, twice runner-up in the world driver's championships for Williams, is on a full-time contract, dividing his time between racing, testing and helping the experts while acting as Williams' public face, talking to sponsors and their guests and making the witty speeches. This makes far more demand on his time than sixteen very public appearances at the wheel of a car.

Travel costs are another enormous burden. There was a time when teams negotiated individually with each Grand Prix organizer. If they did not get what they wanted, they did not turn up. There were only fifteen cars at Grands Prix on occasions! Now each team has a contract with Formula One Constructors Association (FOCA) guaranteeing to appear at each of the sixteen races and in return are paid a proportion of their travel costs.

Again, money makes money because the more successful the team the more of their costs are paid. Williams receive the expenses of their race team, the transportation costs of two cars and for some of the accompanying freight; more when the race is outside Europe. The team's own share of the bill is still large, and they must pay all of their testing costs at tracks in Britain and France.

It all adds up. Winning the Formula 1 constructor's championship in 1986 cost Williams £10 million. Winning it again in 1987 cost another £10 million. And if the Japanese car manufacturers Honda had not provided the best engines at their own expense as their share of a partnership, each season would have cost between £15 and £20 million. 'Money,' said the late Colin Chapman, founder of Team Lotus, as long ago as 1974, 'is how we keep the score in motor racing.'

It is Frank Williams' job to keep his team's score high in the market place. Head, his technical and engineering director and the only other shareholder, designs the cars, liaises with the drivers and runs the factory. He is an acknowledged leader in his field who would have designed Spitfires in another age. Williams finds him the money to do it, as he has been doing since the two became partners in 1977.

Williams was born to it. A public schoolboy with a good education and well-spoken, he fell in love with the macho world of motor-racing at first sight, after taking six hours to hitchhike sixty miles from Nottingham to a race at Silverstone. After that, apart from a few weeks selling Campbell soups, he never did anything else. He drove saloon cars and finally Formula 3 but never well enough to have a future driving cars. He was smart enough to realize that he was far better at buying and selling them, or, more often, bits of them: gearboxes and carburettors.

It was a trade which kept his own car on the road for a time and later others for his friend Piers Courage, with whom he shared a flat in Harrow. At first it was Formula 3 and 2 cars and finally in 1969 a Brabham in Formula 1. A year later, with money from Italy, Williams bought a De Tomaso car for Courage and in the Dutch Grand Prix he was killed in it. The accident was due to chassis failure and was a huge personal loss to Williams from which he did not recover for years.

Sponsors started coming into the sport in 1968 when Imperial Tobacco created the Gold Leaf team. In 1972, Williams got into the act when he signed an Italian driver who was personally sponsored by Marlboro which brought him their support. But, although he tried several different designers, and their cars, nothing worked for him, as it had with Courage. 'It was the era when everybody laughed when Frank signed a cheque,' says a friend.

In 1975, heavily in debt, he sold his team to an Austrian Canadian, Walter Wolf, who had made his money in oil rigs. Wolf bought the losses, Frank lost his majority shareholding, all control of the team and, for a time, was just a bag carrier for Wolf. Finally, at the beginning of 1977, he gave his notice and formed his own team again, taking Head, a back-room boy at the Wolf team, with him.

They started at a small factory on a trading estate near Didcot beside the M4, buying a March car to fill the gap until Head had designed his own chassis. Frank went off seeking the funds to pay for it, and through a friend in the London gaming world was introduced to an Arab who was spending a lot of money in the clubs. He was staying at the Dorchester Hotel at the time, and Williams had Head paint their car in the Arab's company colours and park it in the forecourt. The Arab wrote out a cheque for £30,000 there and then.

Williams missed the car's first race of the 1978 season. He was in Saudi Arabia persuading the Royal Family to invest in the team to promote Saudi companies. When, in its third race, Head's car finished in the points, the Saudis needed no more persuasion. The team was renamed Saudi-Williams, was painted in the livery of Saudi Airlines, with other Saudi companies taking turns to appear on it bodywork.

Head's design had created a quick car, and a quick and successful car attracts sponsors. Conversely, the Arrow team, which had mediocre cars from the start, have struggled for sponsors and money, and had to sell their shares to stay in the race. Williams has not looked back since that first season. 'The cars have carried my name but they are Patrick's babies,' says Williams.

One Arab led Williams to another, and another. Soon he had cornered the market in them. One, Mansour Ojjeh, had a business called Techniques d'Avant Garde (TAG), a financing house for promising businesses. He put so much into Williams to have TAG's symbol on the car that the team could afford a second car and a second driver, Clay Regazzoni, to support the Australian Alan Jones. That year Regazzoni won Williams his first Grand Prix, and, because of the Saudi involvement, they toasted it in milk. Already TAG was the largest benefactor. Later Ojjeh was to buy a share of the McLaren team and rename it TAG-McLaren.

In 1980 Williams pulled off another coup, getting team sponsorship from Leyland Vehicles by arranging a deal with the Saudis who bought a number of their trucks. Leyland Tractors sponsored a driver and the Austin Rover Group provided road cars. And all with the Williams car powered to victory by Ford Cosworth engines!

The Saudis also provided another contact, the Saudi-division of Mobil Oil, who offered fuel and lubricants, and that led eventually to the present major involvement of the company's world-wide marketing and research division in New York.

Other deals happened by similar chance. Williams, a linguist who counts Italian among his languages, picked up Denim, the Italian men's toiletry brand of Elida-Gibbs. ICI Fibres joined Williams when the Finnish Driver Keke Rosberg came to the team, and stayed with them when he left. And Williams' successes persuaded others to change their loyalty. Barclays, a BAT cigarette brand not sold in Britain, pulled out of a major involvement with the struggling Arrows team to buy a strip at the bottom of the cockpit sides of Williams' cars and identification on drivers' helmets and overalls. That alone cost them £625,000 for the first season. They have expanded for their second.

Each sponsor has a part of the car, and some also have the driver's clothing. In 1987 the sides and rear wings were red and white for Canon, who bought the rights to call the team Canon Williams Honda for three years. The cockpit and engine cover were yellow for ICI, although they sub-let the front wing and plates to their affiliates at every race, and sub-let the cockpit for the races in Monaco, Germany and Detroit. Then there are the Barclays strips and the Mobil name on the front cowling and the side of the cockpit.

The 1987 Williams car in its commercial livery, every millimetre of bodywork sold to a sponsor.

The size of each company logo (to the last millimetre) and its location on the car is part of their contract. If Head happens to add so much as a two millimetre bubble on the side of the engine that was not on the original plans, as Williams' executive Peter Windsor puts it: 'everything hits the fan'. Mobil's marketing department spent hours discussing which bit of the 'M' in Mobil on one side of the car and which bit of the blue strip on the other would be left out because of an extended bit of fairing.

None of this work can be done on the cars until Head has finished designing the body shell, often on the eve of the season. To avoid the hotch-potch of colours and logos clashing, a design studio in London co-ordinates the work.

Windsor, a former journalist, and, until recently, Sheridan Thynne have been employed by Williams since 1979 to keep sponsors happy. They attend the sponsor's hospitality areas at Grands Prix, answer their guests' questions, arrange trips for them to paddock and pits, and introduce them to the drivers. They organize visits by groups of sponsors' clients or employees to the Didcot factory or a testing track.

Typical of the promotional use sponsors make of their involvement with the team was an eve-of-race function Canon put on at Loews Hotel in Monte Carlo for forty VIPs at which Piquet talked them through a lap of the circuit and signed autographs. 'We can't guarantee sponsors that the team will win but we can make sure they get value for money even when we lose,' says Windsor. 'There is an immense incompatibility in the normal way between men like Patrick Head who make racing what it is and those who pay for them to do it. It's our job to keep them both happy.'

Canon widely promote their involvement with the team. When their EOS camera was launched in Britain, the advertising campaign featured the Williams car with the slogan 'The Fastest. It Wins Hands Down. The Best. And that's only the autofocus.' They also do an independent deal with FOCA to build camera towers at seven races and park their magnificent hospitality wagon near the pits which gives them more exposure.

Mobil have a direct involvement in the team because their top-grade synthetic oil, available to the general motorist on the petrol station forecourts, is used in the cars, but they use the sponsorship for a massive public relations campaign. Their United Kingdom affiliate, for example, spend five months planning, organizing and booking their hospitality operation around the British Grand Prix at Silverstone. They will have a spare Williams car parked in their marquee there to which more than 500 guests (owners of shipping fleets, motorway stations and major businesses) will be coached or helicoptered over three days of practice sessions and races, to be wined and dined before Mansell briefs them on his drive. Each Mobil affiliate will do the same at their local Grand Prix, and the German company go so far as to sponsor the Grand Prix at Hockenheim.

Mobil also have an arrangement with Williams to bring a dozen guests on a day out to the factory or to the testing at Silverstone and in France. 'A day out to remember', Williams calls it, and it has proved so successful that Mobil organize twenty each year.

ICI do not sell to the public directly, so their approach is different. In Monte Carlo they hired a ship in the harbour, and entertained their customers (the textile and clothing manufacturers who may use their fibres) with a visit from Mansell as the highlight.

But the first reason for the sponsorships is exposure, the massive projection which an association with the sixteen-race Grand Prix circuit guarantees. Every photograph of a Williams driver in his car displays ICI to the world, and every race is televised.

FOCA send their own crew to each race to guarantee exposure, although at most the national host broadcaster offers a world-wide service. Even in the United States, where Formula 1 is not the major sport it is elsewhere, the ABC network annually screens the Monaco race and their sports cable company, ESPN, all the other races. When the independent television company Cheerleader Productions did a survey of the number of times the name Canon was seen at the 1986 British Grand Prix, and compared it with commercially-bought air-time, they discovered that the company had received five times the value of their annual investment with Williams from that one race. And there were fifteen others!

Williams do get some return from their successes in prize

money, particularly at races such as Silverstone, Monza and Monaco, which are promoted by established clubs rather than at the eight races FOCA underwrite. The difference in prize money between Monaco and Belgium may be forty per cent but even in a successful season it produces only about ten per cent of Williams' overall budget.

The company also have an enormous quarter-scale wind tunnel at Didcot which they rent out to non-competitive teams, like those building cars for the Indianapolis 500. But the income is tiny because Head's own work is so demanding of the tunnel's time. 'There are not enough hours in the day for Patrick and his design team to do all they have to do,' says Windsor.

'We don't have any real income other than that from our sponsors. That's how we survive to go racing, and that's how important they are to us,' says Windsor. 'We need their money up front and preferably on a long-term basis. We could patent our technology and sell it but we don't because in racing it would be defeating the objective of beating everyone else, and we exist for that single purpose. To spend valuable time doing anything which would deflect us from that priority is a waste of time.'

Head has had far more responsibility since Williams drove his car off a French road on his way from a testing session, and survived only as a quadraplegic, paralysed from the shoulders down and able to use his biceps but not his triceps. It means he can bring his hand to his face to feed himself but has no control over the movement of the hand. He wears weighted gloves to stop the hands wind-milling when he lifts his arms.

His office has been adapted to take his wheelchair, and there is a special multi-gym in one corner for him to build up what muscles he can use, and, incredibly, he comes to the office every day and to all the races. Before the accident he had a habit of timing every part of his life. He allowed himself just thirty minutes in August 1974, to race to a Registry Office to get married. Now he is forced to exercise more patience but he still times himself. It takes him ninety minutes to wash and dress in the mornings now, and 'what seems forever to put on my tie.'

He was late for a practice session at Spa in 1987 for the first time in his life, an important point to him, but to his team the presence of a man who was close to death three times during his twelve weeks in hospital is enough to inspire. He takes what he calls the 'longer, broader view', listening and making the value judgements, the commercial decisions. And, while everybody at Didcot calls him Frank (and he knows all their first names), he says with determination: 'I'm not a passenger here. I'm the guvnor.'

But, in a well-ordered team, his most important role is being Frank Williams, remarkable figurehead of the organization, and thanking his lucky stars that he had had the foresight to structure the company so well before the accident that it continued without him to win nine Grand Prix races during the 1986 season.

Head is the one at the sharp end, a man who did not come to the job direct from a design college but from racing Clubmen cars himself and building things with his own bare hands; from the machinery to the fabricating. He and John Barnard, the chief designer for Ferrari, are head and shoulders above the rest of their generation. Head gets a salary as a director but nothing compared to the sums paid to the men who drive his cars. Yet they would never win a race without him. 'He's more critical to our team than any manager of a soccer club,' says Windsor.

It was the realization of this importance that persuaded Williams in 1978 to put the word Engineering rather than Racing in his company title for the first time. 'It's about cars first, drivers second and, thirdly, the money to put it all together; but above all engineering,' says Williams.

Head is so important that the drivers' compatibility with him is crucial to their selection. All must have technical experience because to build them better cars Head must have accurate feedback. He de-briefs the drivers for up to two hours after every practice session and race, when thoughts are freshest in their minds. Mansell is famous for calling Head from wherever he is in the world when a thought about the car enters his head.

In 1989, when the rules change to bar the use in Grand Prix racing of turbo-charged engines and the normally-aspirated hold sway again with their smaller, 510 brake-horse-power, the demands on Head's department may be less and certainly the team's costs will be reduced.

For the moment, however, money makes their world go round, and for the 1988 season Williams found themselves needing more than ever because of the ending of their agreement with Honda. Other companies offered them their engines free in exchange for promotion of their name on the car's body, but Williams chose the more expensive option of paying for the development of a normally-aspirated engine in conjuction with an engineer-friend of Head's, John Judd.

Williams' reputation for success ensured that there was no shortage of companies willing to take Honda's place on the car, and it will continue to do so as long as motor racing offers the exposure it does at present.

'If the markets collapse and the sponsors have to pull out, Williams wouldn't disappear ,' says Windsor. 'It wouldn't be as it is now. We would have to prune. But we would still go racing. It may be with one car, one driver and only half a dozen races each year, but we would be there. Frank would never retire to Monte Carlo and live happily ever after. He would be bored out of his mind. His life, our lives, are about coming here every day and preparing to go racing.'

One of the perks of sponsorship – Len Owen, special events director of Gallaher, gets to present a prize to Seve Ballesteros. Watching is Gallaher chairman Stuart Cameron, who created the company's sponsorship division in 1970.

9
THE SPONSOR

THE FIRST sponsor of sport was probably a Roman patrician currying favour with his Emperor by underwriting a day of blood-letting in the Colosseum. He would have regarded himself as the patron of the games but since he was seeking a return on investment, he was being no more philanthropic than any of today's commercial sponsors.

The definition of sporting sponsorship, arrived at by the 1982 Committee of Inquiry into the field which was chaired by former Sports Minister Denis Howell, puts the patrician in his place. 'Sponsorship is the support of a sport, sports event, sports organization or competitor by an outside body or person for the mutual benefit of both parties.'

From the patrician and for the next 2,000 years the industry progressed little. An Australian caterer, Spiers and Pond, did underwrite the cost of England's first cricket tour in 1861 although it might be stretching the definition to class as a sponsor a company who walked away with £11,000 in profit. In the 1930s the health sales company, Kruschen, tried a similar route by sponsoring the first British rugby league tour of Australia. Not much notice was taken of it.

Twenty years later the scene had changed little. In 1957 the only sponsored sports event shown on television was the Whitbread Gold Cup, for which the brewery paid racing £4,250. As recently as 1971, the Sports Council calculated that the sponsorship of sport amounted to no more than £2.5 million.

What a difference today. Try to think of one sport covered by television that is not sponsored, and remember that BBC alone, by their own estimate, showed 1,500 hours of sports during 1987, twenty per cent of their entire output. The sports pages of today's newspapers mention almost as many company names as the Stock Exchange listings. Is there any event so small and so trivial now that there is not some company willing to sponsor?

Little can move on the sports scene without some part of its anatomy being plastered with a company's name. Footballers proclaim their sponsors' names on their shirts, skiers on their helmets and goggles, athletes on their vests, boxers on their shorts and tennis players on their sleeves. Formula 1 racing drivers wear theirs everywhere that is visible.

Hardly a national institution remains which has not had its title usurped. Cricket's Test matches bowed to business first, then the Boat Race, the Grand National and the Derby and, most recently, after more than a century of being supported only by its public, the FA Cup. Even Wimbledon and golf's British Open have succumbed discreetly behind the scenes and only Royal Ascot and the Royal Henley Regatta remain, prim and proper in their rejection of the sponsors' shilling.

During the last two decades not even the property market can equal the rise of almost one hundred fold in the value of sports sponsorship in Britain. In 1988 it was anticipated that not less than £200 million would be invested in sports sponsorships by more than 2,000 companies. These companies would be advised on how sponsorship fitted into their marketing objectives by more than 100 specialist agencies.

Sponsorship, which once fought for crumbs from the advertising department's budget, has become the fourth strong arm of marketing; a critical cousin to the advertising sales promotion and public relations departments which form the marketing mix. The royal seal of approval was given in 1986 when Saatchi and Saatchi moved into the market with a division called Sponsorship in Business.

The Confederation of British Industry also recognized it in 1987 when it said: 'Increasingly, large and small companies are coming to realize that they can strengthen their reputation, enhance their community standing, reach their target audience, support their marketing objective and even motivate employees through the use of skilled sponsorship.' And when sponsorship has been recognized as doing all that, it is not surprising that in the first six months of 1987, 118 companies announced new sponsorships, totalling more than £25 million, while only fifteen dropped out.

Len Owen is not a Roman patrician but he did come into the business of sponsorship before almost everybody else. He has been a sponsor's man for as long as his rivals can remember, responsible for one of the largest sponsorship budgets for seventeen years as Special Events Director of the tobacco company Gallaher, makers of Benson and Hedges, Silk Cut and Senior Service brands of cigarette.

When Owen attended his first sponsored event, the Senior Service tournament at Dalmahoy in Scotland, there were no sponsorship agencies because there were no marketing objectives. Companies sponsored because one of the senior executives or directors liked the sport, or who had a daughter who did. Gallaher had a director who was a member of the Jockey Club, so they sponsored the odd horse race. Another director had a yacht and suggested it would be a jolly good idea to sponsor sailing because of Senior Service's nautical image. Each senior executive pushed his own favourite. 'There was no policy of sponsorship,' says Owen. 'It was all ad hoc.'

Golf was promoted because Binnie Clark, one of the executives, happened to love it. Not only did he push for the company to sponsor it but he wanted to run the event himself. There was no specific department then to oppose his wishes, and the advertising department certainly did not want to know about it, so he had his way. He turned out to be one of golf's great innovators. He put up British golf's first tented village, its first grandstands and, later, became its first sponsor to pay a four figure cheque. When he retired from the company, he became secretary of Bognor Regis Golf Club and became consultant to the Ford Motor Company's amateur tournament.

Men like Owen, who was one of the company's young sales managers, were roped in to help. Owen did not object. He happened to like golf as much as Clark. When Clark could not swing it with Owen's bosses, Owen would take a week's holiday to help him. 'It was all terribly informal,' he recalls. 'Hard work but nobody at the top of the company seemed to be greatly interested. They studied them after the event to see whether they had been worthwhile but we got into them on somebody's whim.'

That meant Gallaher were into a variety of sponsorships without any clear objectives. Many 'one-horse races' under the corporate banner of Gallaher created little impact and were not repeated.

Most, however, were under the Senior Service banner because that was the company's biggest selling brand. When, in 1966, the bottom fell out of the market for plain cigarettes, all sponsorship was abandoned. Gallaher simply stopped spending on sponsorship and sales promotion. Owen, who by that time had become a sales promotions manager, was dispatched back into a sales job in Manchester because no promotions were being done.

In the early sixties Gallaher had bought Benson and Hedges, a small upmarket filter-tip brand, and just as plain cigarettes lost popularity, B & H gained it. By 1970 it was obvious to the company that this was the brand, properly marketed, that could be the company leader. Sponsorship, decided Stuart Cameron, the general manager of marketing, was part of the mix. Owen, then a sales manager again, was invited back from Manchester to mastermind a new department as special events manager reporting to Cameron. The department eventually became him, an assistant, Nick Hill, and a secretary. 'I think I was remembered because I'd been willing to turn out in the old days,' he says.

It was that partnership of Cameron and Owen that laid the foundation of a policy towards sponsorship within the company which has never changed. 'Never again would we sponsor anything because somebody or their wife wanted it, although occasionally I've had to fight off the odd suggestion that we should,' says Owen.

The Cameron – Owen objectives in 1971 were enshrined into company policy. Most have remained relevant today. They were:

1. To form an extension of the main advertising campaign.

2. To establish corporate identity, linking that identity with exellence.

3. To consolidate name and brand awareness leading ultimately to increased sales.

There were the ten commandments to support them; criteria to be applied to every sponsorship. These were:

1. Only major activities in sport.

2. Guaranteed national television.

3. Guaranteed national radio and national press. ('Two and three were critical and still are,' says Owen.)

4. Total name identification. ('We'd consider no event unless our name was in the title.')

5. Simplicity of title.

6. Prestige event.

7. No multi-sponsorship. ('Never have other sponsors involved as co-sponsor.')

8. No fragmentation. ('Stick to one event in a sport, not spread yourself thinly.')

9. Events should be cost-effective. ('Where possible we should own the events and get a return on them.')

10. Right target market. ('Up market.')

The objectives have never changed and the criteria have altered only slightly; and because Cameron rose through the company to become chairman there has been continued support at the highest level for the programme and its objectives. 'From the start he saw sponsorship as part of a mix, not something which had to justify itself on its own.'

That was the dilemma that companies which were considering entering sponsorship wrestles with in the seventies. How do you justify sponsorship? Did it sell the product? It was the wrong question for which there was no true answer.

Many other companies put their advertising departments or agents in charge of it, and neither wanted to lose any of their budget. The agents received seventeen and a half per cent of all they spent above the line and there was no similar incentive to commit part of the budget to sponsorship. 'I can remember young marketing men turning up at sponsorship seminars, noses in the air, all very disdainful,' says Owen.

Sponsorship in most large companies had to fight for every penny. Cameron always saw it just as one facet of marketing. 'I could never prove to him the value of any individual event, from my first day,' says Owen. 'It increases awareness of Benson and Hedges. That's all we can prove. At the same time I am running a high profile sports sponsorship, the advertising department might be running a £1 million campaign. How can you tell which of them is selling our products?

'We measure it against our objectives, national press, radio and television, and we measure it day in, day out. We have this very unsophisticated cottage industry of people who monitor everything, who are employed to watch television and award points. At the end of a year I can give a figure for the number of hours and minutes Benson and Hedges has appeared on TV at its events. It doesn't prove anybody has bought one more cigarette.

'Not even locally can we do that. If we have an event in York, say, and sales there rise, is it the event, or perhaps the event has just drawn people from outside York into the city. Or perhaps we had an advertising campaign running at the time. You must not judge sponsorship by sales. Awareness is a far better guide.'

Some agencies go further than B & H's monitoring and use a formula against paid advertising to show whether the number of mentions and sightings a sponsor obtains against what a sponsor has paid is cheaper than paid advertising time. 'It's an attempt to be sophisticated without it meaning anything,' is Owen's judgement. 'You simply cannot separate sponsorship from the mix.'

For a tobacco manufacturer, whose advertising outlets are restricted by the government, sponsorship is the most effective way into television, radio and the national press. The estimated 400 hours of television time their events receive in a year is sufficient justification for the millions spent. It is a bonus that the companies may also entertain clients at their events, distribute their products and be seen putting money into something socially acceptable. But none of those reasons are enough on their own for a tobacco manufacturer. Exposure which increases awareness is the single reason why sport receives sponsorship from these companies.

Non-tobacco sponsors give more importance to the other aspects. James Capel, the stockbrokers, poured £250,000 into yachting in the year after the Big Bang in the City and a good part was justified by the chance it gave to meet potential clients at places like Cowes. Even so, Capel were quick to admit that a name mention in a national newspaper connecting them with the sport was worth ten full-page advertisements.

For the tobacco man, the forbidden fruit of television is the attraction. Only about one in ten of sponsors of British sport (excluding horse racing) get television coverage, but all the tobacco sponsors chose events which are shown. Hardly surprising then that in 1986 five of the top six in terms of hours on the screen were tobacco companies and that about sixteen per cent of all televised sport was tobacco sponsored. All insist on contracts with the governing bodies of the sports spelling out in detail the time which the governing body's own contract with television will give them.

In the early days Benson and Hedges decided that there was room for minor sports in their sponsorship package as long as B & H were wholly dominant in the sport and there was no obvious connection to the young or to schools. Hockey and squash were the two sports chosen. For six years the company sponsored every major event in hockey, indoors and outdoors. 'It was a lot of activity but all small beer and it was not achieving for us pro rata to the effort in manpower. We were out and about every weekend, giving it hours of our executive time but not getting a great return,' says Owen.

Squash was abandoned first because Benson and Hedges never felt comfortable with it. 'It was a pure physical activity and we were slightly incongruous in it. I always felt I was in the wrong place. You could have a cigarette when playing golf or cricket and even the hockey crowd were a cosmopolitan bunch who enjoyed the odd drink and a cigarette. Squash was more obsessive.'

The company still do non-televised events, such as fly fishing championships and club tennis, but these events are organized on smaller budgets by the marketing department with the different objective of making the product available and being seen to be interested in the grass roots of sport. The special events department handle only the televised occasions.

Golf was the only other sport B & H sponsored in that first year of 1971. It was an international open event at the Fulford Club in York and has been an annual event since, moving once, but returning after a year to York. It was the year it moved that Owen lost television coverage for the first time. 'That is a traumatic experience for a sponsor,' says Owen. 'For a tobacco company sponsor, it is a catastrophe.'

ITV had contracted to cover the event and had laid miles of

their cables at the St Mellion course and rigged their scaffolding and cameras when producer Lawrie Higgins arrived to say it was off. There was a strike.

'The two brothers, Hermon and Martin Bond, who owned the course, were in tears,' says Owen. 'It had been their big chance to get it known.' Owen says he needed a large drink himself to get over the shock.

From the start, Owen had decided to take on an outside agency to assist his tiny staff. In 1971, West Nally Ltd were chosen, partly because of its chairman Peter West's knowledge of sport. 'They were the arms and legs and creativity,' he says, 'and with so few of us in-house we needed all three.' Ten years later when Karen Earl, the account director at West Nally, broke away to form her own company, Owen kept the account with her. Now she also handles all Gallaher's Silk Cut sponsorships.

'I've always favoured working with agencies. For one thing they are specialists, and to us it is no different to the ad agencies we employ. They also mean you don't have to take on huge staffs in-house to launch sponsorships when you don't know how long they may survive.'

The staffing needs are enormous because B & H chose to run several of their sponsored events themselves. Their tennis tournament has fifteen paid specialists on its tournament committee under the chairmanship of Owen, who are responsible for such elements as ball boys, umpires, transport and players. Owen is again director of the golf tournament but he employs a tournament administrator who is resident in York for four weeks before the tournament and one after it.

Cricket, on the other hand, is the responsibility of the Test and County Cricket Board and Owen was prepared to forego a closer involvement because of his conviction that it was right for the B & H image. It would have been his choice to launch the programme in 1971 but, unlike the three other sports he chose, the cricket tournament took a year of negotiation and planning, with West using all his contacts at Lord's before the Benson and Hedges Cup, a one-day competition for the early part of the summer, could be launched in 1972.

Cricket had had a successful one-day knock-out competition since 1963 when Gillette first put £6,500 into a contest for the seventeen first-class counties. Henry Garnett, their managing director, perhaps typically of the time, saw his money only as an insurance against bad weather for cricket, and asked nothing in return. It was a cross between patronage and sponsorship at a time when managing directors still went into the sports of their liking.

Their motivation for the sponsorship changed over the years but they never promoted the razor blade connection strongly and eventually the public were associating the Gillette Cup with cricket but not with razor blades. In 1981 they drew the line at increasing their fee beyond £130,000 and withdrew. National Westminster immediately picked up the event for a fee of £250,000, index-lined to inflation.

The Benson and Hedges Cup is now seventeen years old and flourishing, and Owen sees no problems for his company in the name association. 'Personally I am very happy doing the same thing again and again as long as we are refining and improving. What we do now are events that have matured and grown but I don't think they have lost what they offered us in the first place. They still meet all our criteria.'

Cricket is expensive sponsorship. By 1986 B & H were paying £400,000 to the Test and County Cricket Board and their cricket was televised for thirty-one hours fifty-five minutes, ranking eighth among televised events in time but nearly the most expensive in terms of cost per hour. Their own snooker tournament, The Masters, gained them nearly five more hours for half as much money.

Cricket gives them the receipts from the sale of 20,000 souvenir programmes which Benson and Hedges produce themselves, but the sport takes all income from gate receipts at the Benson and Hedges matches. On the other hand, Benson and Hedges own their snooker tournament, as they do their Grand Prix tennis tournament at Wembley and the golf at Fulford, so the admission fees go into their kitty.

Admission fees make an enormous difference to the cost effectiveness of sponsorship. Attendance at the 1986 tennis tournament produced receipts of £600,000, of which Wembley take forty per cent in lieu of the usual hire charge. At Fulford, in 1987, receipts from spectators topped £100,000 for the first time.

'Clark adopted this policy of promoting and sponsoring our own events in the early days of Senior Service,' says Owen. 'We made peanuts from it then but when Benson and Hedges started we actually looked at how much we wanted to be involved before we went into a sport. Usually we asked if the event would exist without us. If not, we promoted.'

Curiously, no other sponsoring company in Britain is known to do the same. The other give their money to the sport and let them get on with it, devoting their efforts exclusively to promoting the link. 'I don't know why because to me the involvement is enriching,' says Owen. 'It's not a sense of power for me but it is very satisfying for the company. We are not the guests when we sponsor but the hosts. At our cricket final we are made very welcome and have many friends at Lord's but it is different somehow when you are the guests for the day. At golf and tennis and snooker, people are our guests. We feel more at home.'

Not that a sponsor who is also promoting has much time for relaxation. Owen is the tournament director at tennis and golf and responsible for all that goes on. How many sponsors would have been running around Wembley Arena with a fire extinguisher as Owen was the first year of the tennis tournament when a BBC television cable in the roof caught fire.

'I remember running for the extinguisher and being told by a commissioner that I had to sign for it. I refused but then the thing wouldn't work anyway. It was a rotten start. The sprinkler system rained all over the brand new carpets we had laid in our hospitality boxes.' The tennis has had more than its share of problems. Another year the roof sprung a leak and the ball boys had to be armed with mops to keep the court dry. And there was a famous occasion when Arthur Ashe twisted his neck trying to manoeuvre himself into Gerry Williams' tiny radio commentary box to do an interview, and had to scratch from the event.

As director, Owen is responsible also for recruiting the star players. The Professionals Golfers Association (PGA) and the Association of Tennis Professionals (ATP) guarantee him an entry, but three times each year he travels to America to 'chat up' the names he wants to compete.

After so long in the game, Owen knows most of those he wants personally. Golfer Lee Trevino became a good friend, coming five times, and he has always felt able to approach the likes of Jimmy Connors directly. 'Men like them expect to negotiate with the top man at any tournament.' Private deals are outlawed by ATP. What a tournament offers its star it must offer the other players, but in any case Owen's experience is that it is not possible to offer enough money to tempt the superstars to go where they would prefer not to be. 'Once a player has a certain earning potential, it's the quality of life that's important, the little thing that make his lot easier, like the physiotherapy and the stringing service, the practice courts, the courtesy car laid on. In our case, a lot of players like to be in London a few weeks before Christmas because their wives want to do their shopping. Little things like that are as important as money.' In recent years B & H have even built a well-furnished marquee behind the court at Wembley which is exclusively reserved for players and their relatives and friends.

The company was able to pursue its policy of running its own events because its events were bespoke sponsorships, created for them and to suit them. Their show jumping (now sponsored by Silk Cut), the Grand Prix tennis, and horse racing's Gold Cup at York, were others. Horse racing was dropped after a decade but the others have stood the test of time – tennis is the youngest at a sprightly twelve years old – probably because they were custom-made from the start. Now, with sporting calendars clogged with events, it is not possible to introduce more and the policy for Silk Cut in the 1980s has been to take what they need off the peg, like their Rugby League Challenge Cup sponsorship.

Sometimes the Cameron–Owen criteria cost them major events. They were involved in snooker before the boom with the world championships now sponsored by rivals Embassy. It is the big one which got away from Owen. Gallaher sponsored it in 1973 and 1974 in Manchester under the banner of Park Drive. The first year the tournament did not get a minute of television, and the second year it received only a few hours. 'The total prize money then does not match the prize Steve Davis now wins,' says Owen.

Then the championships were sent to Australia for a year and when they returned Benson and Hedges, in line with their policy to create what they wanted, had started their own Masters tournament. 'Because we never allow ourselves to be spread across a sport, we passed up the chance to get the World's back,' says Owen. Embassy had more than 120 hours of exposure sponsoring the world championships in 1986, three times that of the B & H Masters.

In Britain, direct sponsorship fees paid to sport rose above £160 million in 1987. They remained small compared to companies' budgets for press and television advertising, barely five per cent of them, but the indirect spend on sponsorship when the support of public relations, promotion and advertising are taken into account may be at least double that, something now in the region of £300 million.

That figure is dwarfed by the American sponsorship market. It has been estimated by the marketing industry there that 3,400 US companies spent $1.35 billion during 1987, and the largest growth area was in the support of events.

Four years earlier US companies has spent almost $500 million on sponsoring star players, in endorsement and advertising contracts. That figure has changed little since, while the sponsorship of events has quadrupled. The cigarette giant Philip Morris is now said to be spending $85 million; RJR Nabisco $58 million, and brewers Anheuser-Busch $50 million.

Sport does not benefit in direct financial terms to this extent. Companies are spending increasingly large proportions of their sponsorship budgets on buying television air time for their sponsored sport, something not permitted yet in Britain but widely accepted in the US. Mobil Oil 'sponsored' the showing there of athletic's Grand Prix final in Rome by buying the television network's commercial time. Mercedes did the same to persuade NBC to screen a show-jumping event they were sponsoring, and although audience rates were almost non-existent, NBC were happy with what was described as their 'most profitable' sports show.

The tobacco industry in the early 1970s may have contributed as much as one third of all sponsorship in Britain because so few companies in other industries were interested. Colin Chapman wrote a thousand letters in his search for a sponsor for his Lotus Formula 1 racing team but only John Player replied.

Today, the industry's total spend annually in Britain is a closely guarded secret. It is probably in the region of £12 million. That maintains its position as the largest spending sector but it is less than ten per cent of the vastly increased pool of sponsorship and far less than the industry would be spending without the restrictions imposed by the government.

These restrictions are known, perhaps euphemistically, as the industry's voluntary code of contract and regulate what may be sponsored and how it should be sponsored. The bottom line is that is forbids the industry from spending any more in real terms than it did in 1976.

The 'declarable' figure is less than £12 million because the companies' spending on agency-employed personnel, agency fees, research and hospitality do not have to be included in their restricted budgets; but it does have to include all their revenues from sponsorships. So Benson and Hedges do not gain any advantage in that sense from promoting events from which they may obtain a secondary income from attendance and programme receipts. 'It means we have to outlay less for the same sponsorship but does not mean we can spend more,' explains Owen. 'We've always stayed within the code as a matter of company policy. It became the eleventh of our commandments.'

The original figures for each tobacco company were based on what each spent on their sponsorship in 1976. It seemed a reasonable method of distribution. 'After all, we could hardly argue that we needed more because when we could have spent more we hadn't,' says Owen. 'It was never much of a problem at the time because we were having a lot a trouble justifying our level of spending to our own marketing men anyway. We lived quite happily within that amount for some years.'

The code covers only that part of a tobacco company's budget spent within the United Kingdom. So what support multi-national brands such as Marlboro and Camel give to racing teams performing abroad is outside the limitations. When John Player sponsored the British Lotus team in the mid-1970's, they had to declare only one-eighth of their sponsorship because only two of the sixteen Grand Prix races took place in Britain and the rest was funded by John Player's international owner, BAT. R.J. Reynolds, whose Camel brand has since taken over the Lotus sponsorship, needs to use a measure of only one-sixteenth now that only one Grand Prix is held in Britain.

Owen believes that most tobacco companies would spend more now if the restrictions were relaxed. 'All our brands want to do more because they realize how effective it is,' he says. It is generally thought that the tobacco companies are spending to the limits of their agreement with the possible exception of John Player who have cut back since their take-over by Hanson Trust.

But expansion of sponsorship programmes is impossible, and most levels find it difficult even to maintain programmes at present levels within the limitations. A tobacco sponsor like Gallaher has to live with the inflationary spiral of prize money in the sports they support when their own budget can exceed what they spent in 1976 only by the margin of the nation's inflation, a notional statistic to the McEnroes and Lendls of the sporting world who are unwilling to accept any limitation on their own demands. Prize money for B & H International tennis tournament was increased under Grand Prix rules by almost one-third, a total of $100,000, between 1986 and 1988, while the Gallaher budget increased by barely ten per cent. Prize money has almost trebled since the tournament began.

They pay up or get out. There are any number of sponsors queuing for competitions which become available, and sports may be disinclined in the future to negotiate within the restrictions imposed on B & H by their industry's agreement. 'It's very difficult for us,' admits Owen.

Television and tobacco have lived together uneasily for some years. In 1986 restrictions on their events were tightened by individual producers. Rothmans were forced to remove blue, the colour of its packs, from the surrounds at its snooker tournament, and Gallaher had to overpaint its yellow umpire chairs red at the B & H tennis tournament. Owen, however, is confident that they will be still co-existing well beyond his retirement in 1991.

Benson and Hedges' contracts with the Test and County Cricket Board, the PGA and ATP, all of which guarantee the sponsor television coverage, end in 1989, and its contract with the World Professional Billiards and Snooker Association in February 1990. But there were meetings during the winter of 1987 at which television's representatives promised that present events will not be abandoned because of the particular product of their sponsors.

'Certainly all the governing bodies we deal with want us to stay with them,' says Owen. 'We are among the more professional people they deal with, and we add to and subtract nothing from their events.'

But Silk Cut have been forced to drop out of their partnership with the annual Country Music festival at Wembley because television was unhappy with a tobacco sponsor, and television is making it clear that they will not entertain coverage of any new sporting events which have tobacco sponsors.

Many marketing departments have had internal discussions about the future role of television in their sponsorships. Most would continue without it but in a very different way, seeking exposure through events with larger crowds, greater number of participants or the potential for promotion through the written press. Already Silk Cut have a club tennis event which involves 1,000 clubs and B & H have a trout fishing event with a large entry.

No sponsoring company in Britain gets that close to the establishment of television to know its mind. None are allowed face-to-face negotiations even with television because the British networks have made a point of dealing only with the governing bodies of sport. It is a reasonable principle but on occasions it is taken to extreme lengths, as with B & H's tennis tournament for which the BBC prefer to talk terms with the Association of Tennis Professionals (ATP) in America than with the British promoter and sponsor, because ATP is, in the BBC's eyes, a governing body.

But for the moment television holds all the cards in a seller's market, which is hardly surprising when a sponsor such as Volvo reveals that the television projection it gained through sponsorship of international tennis's Grand Prix was worth $18 million in 1986 for an outlay of $3 million.

Next to that, aspects of sports sponsorship such as the entertainment of clients and live crowd as a captive audience are not highly regarded. 'They are important but not sufficiently important to help us decide whether to sponsor an event,' says

Owen. 'But in five years' time, yes, that could be a more important consideration.'

An event then might justify itself to a cigarette company as a low cost entertainment. Gallaher do it now on occasions such as Wimbledon where they have to spend about £2,000 for a table for eight for one day. At their own events, such as the tennis tournament at Wembley, they can wine and dine guests in armchair comfort in carpeted boxes at courtside for a sixth of that price.

Not that it will matter much to Owen himself. The golf course is beckoning him to work on his ten handicap. He will retire in 1991 after thirty-seven years with Gallaher; his whole working life since finishing his National Service in the Royal Navy. He was interested then only in the car which went with the salesman's job, but to be a sponsor's man has had other compensations, not least for Owen himself the odd round of golf with stars like Lee Trevino and Bernard Langer.

In the bad, old days of sponsorship, before marketing men and media evaluations, Owen, you sense, would have been one of those sponsoring golf for no other reason than personal preference. He smiles at the suggestion. 'It's a good thought. Would have done wonders for my handicap.'

The new team – Patrick Nally (left) and Alan Pascoe, two of the sportsworld's leading marketing agents.

10

THE MARKETING MAN

IN BRITAIN, in the sixties and seventies, sport was the arena for the young buccaneers of the marketing world, a new world where the established advertising and public relations companies never trod. Small companies, often one man and a secretary with a single client, came and went as fast as sports changed their sponsors.

Sport was desperate for money and there were few family heirlooms too precious to pawn. The sports marketing agents were the brokers, putting together marriages of sport and sponsor for an introduction fee and often staying around for a further fee to play a role in making them work.

Cricket sold its Test matches to an insurance company, swimming its national team to an oil company and tennis its oldest international competition to a Japanese multi-national electronics giant. Even soccer's World Cup went to a soft drinks bottler.

All these sponsorships had something in common, apart from the money which they generated. A Londoner, Patrick Nally, negotiated their sale. In the sixties and seventies he was one of the young men who led the way, and in the eighties he was one of the few who survived; bruised and bloodied and a lot greyer, but still in the game in the top division.

Today Nally is managing director of Pascoe Nally International, the international sponsorship division of the advertising giant WCRS Group. He is a married man with children and a splendid house on the Thames, and an established figure in the marketing world. But in those early days of sponsorship, when men like him were inventing the genre, he was the international cavalier for whom the British market was a base from which to conquer the world.

In one three-year period he was in the air between countries more days of each year than he was on the ground. He lived in hotels or company flats, owned no property of his own and managed in four years to put less than 10,000 miles on the clock of his Mercedes. 'There wasn't time in my schedule to drive anywhere,' he says.

He was a fast-moving, fast-talking salesman with nothing more tangible to peddle to major corporations than the idea that sport could be a medium for communication, as sponsorship, or advertising or just public relations. But the world listened, and the client list was impressive: Ford Motor Company, Benson and Hedges, Kraft Foods, Green Shield Trading Stamps, Cornhill Insurance and Esso, in Britain; Coca-Cola, NEC, Canon, Seiko, and Adidas, among others, abroad.

Necessity being the mother of invention he would create an event where there was none to suit a sponsor. Cricket's Benson and Hedges Cup, gymnastics' and swimming's World Cups, soccer's World Youth Tournament and athletics' former Golden Series were all creations to fill a sponsor's – and, occasionally, a sport's – needs.

Sports desperate to expand would use him as a salesman to market their development. He raised 130 million Swiss francs so that FIFA could expand their World Cup finals from sixteen national teams to twenty-four. He found another $34 million from marketing so that the International Amateur Athletic Federation could stage their first world championships in 1983. He came up with the sponsorship and advertising which launched rugby union's first World Cup in 1987. At the same time he was marketing agent for the world governing bodies of soccer, athletics, swimming, gymnastics and volleyball, and his understanding and appreciation of the politics of international sport is second to none.

Yet what drove him was not a love of sport, but a fascination with selling. Before he had left school at sixteen, he had gone door-to-door in West London, selling his services and those of a friend as a car washer, and he traded second-hand records in Shepherd's Bush market. His first full-time job was with the public relations division of the advertising company Wasey's, generating publicity for Littlewoods Pools about their big winners. It was a job that demanded only a gift of the gab.

He had learned public relations at his mother's knee – she was to become president of the Institute of Public Relations – but his talent always lay in the selling of innovative ideas more than the execution and administration of the work. 'He was full of ideas and enthusiasm but when he'd done anything once he was bored with it,' says a director of one of his major clients. 'He never wanted to stay with one thing for very long.'

In the early days he was moving fast merely to get places. He was barely twenty when one of Wasey's directors, John Chesney, broke away to form his own company and invited Nally to head his PR arm in conjunction with a friend, TV broadcaster Peter West. The subsidiary was called Peter West and Associates PR Ltd, with Chesney owning a majority and Nally twenty-five per cent. The clients were companies seeking conventional PR help, making anything from extractor fans to taps and showers.

Nally was convinced that the way ahead was specialization. West was a famous sporting broadcaster on cricket and rugby union, and sport looked a likely vehicle. After eighteen months, the two had a difference with Chesney and and broke away to become West and Nally. 'I went to a bank manager at the NatWest to ask for £10,000. I was young and unknown and I needed Peter because he was the name, but he did not want to take any risks. I put up what little collateral I had, and Peter would have lost his hair sooner than he did had he known the risks I was taking.' Years later, when the bank manager retired, Nally sent him a snooker table as a thank-you.

They set up on a floor of 1 New Bond Street in 1969 with a staff of two, equal partners in decision-making but not in equity. They had one client, Green Shield, for whom they sought to cure an image problem by introducing family involvement in a training and junior competitive programme for the Lawn Tennis Association

To start with they traded as West and Nally but the conjunction was dropped when letters arrived addressed to Western Ally or even West End Alley. 'The company was a marriage of Peter's understanding of sport and mine of advertising and PR. He had the contacts within sport and was perceived as trustworthy. I had the ideas. But sport was not always of prime importance. It was simply a medium,' he says.

At the time it was untested and unproven. 'We had no track record and nor did sport.' Very soon they realized that existing events were hard to adapt. 'Press and television did not accept the addition of a sponsor's name to a well-established competition. Events had to be created with the sponsor in mind.' Soon he created packages of new competitions for companies such as Gallaher and Kraft, and a total involvement in youth swimming for Esso.

Sport was grateful for any money, and most accommodating. 'There was no greed, only gratitude. The people running sport were pleasant and friendly and grateful. When they invited you to dinner they'd even offer to pay the bill. Now young marketing agents are regarded as a lesser form of life, like money-lenders.'

West Nally grew to meet the realization of British companies of sports' attractions. None of the six employees at the end of the first year earned more than £1,000, but by the third year there was a staff of twenty-five, some earning ten times that. Jacob de Vries, a BBC executive producer, came to create West Nally management, which represented competitors such as boxers Joe Bugner and John Conteh, athlete David Hemery and snooker's Alex Higgins. A straight PR company was opened and a product-ion division, West Nally Creative. A company promoting snooker, including the world championships, was separated from the mainstream, and new companies called Mr Billiards and Mr Pool were established to sell equipment. Nally even launched his own magazine.

'Quite honestly, we didn't know where we were going. Management of sportsmen conflicted with what we were doing for sport's official bodies, and the magazines and the sale and manufacture of equipment were high risk capital projects. When the three-day week began in Britain, we had letters of revolving credit on Australian banks open for the purchase of equipment there while we couldn't ship the stuff because the British docks were closed. It became a nightmare.' The ancillary operations were all shut down, and attention concentrated again on the thriving sponsorship side.

While in Australia, Nally had taken some PR work for Adidas, helping their swimwear division Arena launch their Mark Spitz range and promoting the company's link with the world record-breaking runner Ron Clarke. It led to more public relations with Adidas promoting a textile range they had created with the Association of Tennis Professionals, and to trips to Landersheim, a village in the rolling Alsace countryside thirty miles from Strasbourg, where Adidas' international division had its head-quarters. It was there that Nally was introduced to Horst Dassler, a meeting which, in the next eight years, was to change the way international sport was financed.

Dassler was the only son of the Adidas founder and responsible for the company's French division and much of its international operation. Where his father had been first a shoe maker, he was, by inclination, a salesman who appreciated that the development of sport throughout the world would increase the size of his own market. He was doing everything in his power to help sport, and with the financial strength of one of Europe's largest private companies behind him, his power was considerable.

Dassler had been approached by Joao Havelange, the new Brazilian president of FIFA, soccer's world governing body, soon after his election in 1974. Havelange had garnered support in the Third World by promising a soccer development programme and a world youth tournament. How could he finance it?

'When I explained what we were doing in Britain, persuading companies to put money into sport for reasons of image, Horst saw the possibilities internationally,' says Nally. They decided to team up to find Havelange his funding, and together created a company based in Monaco, SMPI; Dassler's money and con-tracts allied to Nally's ideas and marketing experience.

Nally himself became a Monte Carlo citizen, buying out West's equity in West Nally Ltd and transforming part of it into a service company for SMPI's international clients. 'SMPI bought all the rights and controls, and fed fees to West Nally, but West Nally always retained its separate shareholders and was never taken over as such,' he says.

'At first it was a mutual aid programme. Havelange needed funds. Dassler was dependent on soccer to sell Adidas equipment but couldn't afford to fund it from the company's budget. So I put forward all Havelange had promised, and a bit more, as a marketing package and presented it to international companies.'

'There was no way the international sports federations, like FIFA, could do it for themselves. They were small outfits then. FIFA was a general secretary, Helmut Kaiser, and a couple of assistants. The International Tennis Federation was David Gray, Shirley Woodhead and a secretary. The International Athletics Federation was John Holt and a secretary. Even the International Olympic Committee was tiny. None had any professional staff and none of them understood what they had to market.'

Today, sports marketing companies who wish to market sport have to guarantee payment in advance. The international federations appreciate the value of what they have. In the mid-1970s the federations had never received offers, did not understand the value of the rights they held and, in many cases, had allowed those rights to be taken from them.

It took Nally fourteen months flying between Rio de Janeiro, Atlanta, Los Angeles, London, New York and Zurich to sell soccer's package to Coca-Cola for an overall figure in the region of $5 million for a four-year involvement. They bought the title sponsorship of the first World Youth Tournament for national teams, under twenty-one, a world-wide development programme using the best coaches, doctors and administrators, and a soccer-skills teaching programme.

Coca-Cola were as new to such sporting packages as FIFA, and not dissimilar to the sports federation in how they were constituted. They had operations in 135 countries, broken down into zones, areas and regions, each with profit centres. 'They could not react at first to it because they had no single corporate body which could. All the franchise and bottling operations were largely autonomous, and every decision was being taken at local affiliate level.'

They was also an American company who did not appreciate the international importance of soccer. Fortunately, the Coca-Cola Corporation in Atlanta had as it director of marketing, Al Kileen. He had worked in Africa and understood the strength of soccer. 'Without his support and his dynamic personality, it would have taken fourteen years to sell it to them,' admits Nally. 'He flew round the world with me telling his people that this was what they were going to do. He was very dogmatic.' It may have helped that he was offering them something for nothing because Atlanta was picking up the bill.

'What FIFA offered and what Coke pushed throught their own organization set a trend for sport and other multi-nationals. It was the beginning of all that has happened to sport since,' says Nally. 'But that first time we were inventing the wheel. Just over-coming the legal side took the lawyers months. The deal almost collapsed five times because of legal complications.

FIFA did not have the staff to devise the programme or administer it. So Adidas found them Sepp Blatter, who had been working for a Swiss watch company, to become their develop-ment officer (now their general secretary) and Klaus Willing, a German who had been involved in the organization of the 1974 World Cup. 'Klaus devised soccer's part, while I wrote the marketing side for Coke.'

With simultaneous announcements of the deal in London, and New York, the first multi-national sponsorship of sport was launched, and with it Nally, at the age of thirty, as the marketing man every international sports federation wanted. 'It sounds easy now. Federations do the work for themselves. But there was no structure or blueprint until we wrote one. It was an unbelievable time. I didn't have a social life for three years.'

Nally's next job was to sort out the commercial problems of the 1978 World Cup finals in Argentina. They had the rights to advertising within the grounds but none of the other rights, even the franchises for the sale of soft drinks. So Coca-Cola loaned FIFA enough to buy the rights back, in return for being the major sponsor. If Nally subsequently managed to bring in other sponsors, as he did, their money would go to Coke to reduce their outlay. 'FIFA had been so lax in their contracts that, technically, any soft-drink manufacturer in Argentina could have used the World Cup logos. We had to sign nearly twenty contracts before we got back Coke's exclusivity. Never again has FIFA released any rights to the World Cup from their central control.'

In Argentina Nally had six major sponsors: including Coca-

Cola, Gillette and Seiko, as well as a host of advertisers paying less for individual advertising boards around the pitches. It was difficult to organize, and his staff were endlessly changing the boards throughout the competition as the meetings of different national teams persuaded different advertisers to buy space.

When, after 1978, Nally brought together soccer's other major competitions: the European Championship, the European Cup and the European Cup-Winners Cup, they had learned from their experience. Companies who wished to advertise around arenas had to buy the complete package: so many boards at each match, distributed according to their positioning for television coverage, and, if they chose, so many opportunities to use the events to entertain. 'The sums were so vast that lots of companies couldn't touch it but it was a lot easier to work with the few who could.'

Soon SMPI was working with soccer, swimming, athletics, volleyball, gymnastics, rowing, tennis and judo. They underwrote the establishment of a headquarters in Monte Carlo for the General Assembly of International Sports Federations and even tried to persuade the International Olympic Committee to move their offices there.

'They were all in the same position. Few of them had any commercial control over their own big event. Cycling could not sell a single advertising board at their 1979 world championship because they had not thought to put them in stadia free of existing boards. Our first job with all of them was educating them how to structure their constitutions where they related to rights for marketing and television.'

The biggest challenge of all was the 1982 World Cup in Spain. The host country had won the rights to stage them for sixteen national teams. Havelange wanted to widen their appeal by increasing it to twenty-four, but to get the proposal passed by FIFA he had to guarantee to pay. So he turned again to Dassler. SMPI guaranteed 130 million Swiss francs. Or Dassler did. 'That's when we started guarantees, the beginning of the nightmare,' says Nally. 'Adidas, literally, were guaranteeing the financial success of a World Cup.

'No sports federation has taken a risk since or appreciated that they must work for their money. They've got into the guarantee syndrome. They'll change nothing to help the marketing of their events unless they are given vast payments in advance as a guarantee of success. Sports federations have used them since to solve their financial problems without ever thinking of the consequences or what it means they must do in return. Often they've blindly sold their souls for short-term success.'

Dassler, of course, had no intention of using Adidas money. It was up to Nally to earn it from others. 'It was such an enormous sum that clearly we needed something different, a new concept. It occured to me that there was nothing more valuable to a company than exclusivity. So that's what I offered them. Each company associated with the World Cup exclusive in its own product category, with few enough categories to give them an additional rarity value. We also gave them a four-year involvement, rather than for the three weeks of the championships.'

It was the most successful marketing operation in the history of any single sport. 'We had to raise 130 million Swiss francs to break even and we raised 134 million francs. I'd saved Horst's guarantee but it wasn't a business proposition. My company was turning over a fortune and making no profit. And it happened with every sport we helped. Horst would make guarantees, helping the federation get back control and become financially secure, but gambling that I could cover them. For me it was a nightmare. My life was devoted to four-year cycles of standing still financially. Everybody's copied the techniques now, the Los Angeles Olympics, the IOC, the IAAF, and all made a fortune. I feel like the navvy whose done all the labouring work digging the foundations.'

Nally broke with Dassler in 1982. It was partly money. They were not making a realistic return. 'Horst's only interest was ensuring he was in the right position with federations, that the people he wanted were elected to the powerful positions and that way Adidas' position as the dominant force in sportswear manufacture was protected. He'd got the power and the influence and Adidas all the credit but he'd done it using other companies' money. It was a hell of an idea and it gave us seven incredible years.'

But there was more to it. Nally was finding it difficult working for three masters: the clients, the federations and for Adidas. 'We could not agree on business ethics. He used to say that I was very Anglo-Saxon and should be more Latin in my outlook. Sponsors were being asked to pay huge amounts not because the product was worth it but because that's what Horst had guaranteed a federation. We said twenty million Swiss francs or no deal to companies for the first international soccer packages simply because that way we could meet a guarantee that had been plucked out of the air. The surprise was that companies agreed but when you talk that big you're talking with the board and chief executives of corporations, not their media departments, and professional considerations can go out of the window and emotion comes in.'

The ethical dangers to sport, says Nally, are serious. 'When sums like $20 million are involved there are pressures which touch on human frailties. Inevitably there has been a tremendous amount of mismanagement of the funds going into sport, both within companies and the sports federations. It was part of the evolution at a time when disciplines were not built in. Companies have come to realize they have to put in the right people and the right controls to safeguard them. I'm not sure sport has.

'It is such a perk to become important in an international sports federation, the influence and power it offers is so great, that the election of people should be scrutinized as closely as any government election.'

Indeed, few people perceive the power of sport now. Coca-Cola used its influence with FIFA to send the World Youth Cup finals in 1985 to the Soviet Union. It was no coincidence that the same year its rival Pepsi Cola's exclusive contract in that country ended, and that Coca-Cola sells now in the Soviet Union. Sport was part of commercial trade.

'Horst and I never fell out, we were too close, and if he was alive today we would still have a lot of feeling for each other. He was the great politician, the head of the big conglomerate, but I was an equal partner in our relationship. He needed money to achieve what he wanted and Adidas money was largely unavailable because the control was with his family. I was the catalyst for him to achieve success outside the family. What I brought to his table was vital and the exchange was equitable. He showed me a side of sport I had never seen and I taught him about international companies.'

SMPI stopped trading in 1982. 'If I'd have known he would die at fifty-one, I'd have stayed with him. He offered me an in and when I said no he told me I was giving up the chance to be the most powerful man in sport. I suppose I could have had it all if I had wanted it, but I wanted to be able to walk tall on both sides of the street. I wanted sport to know that I was trying to do my best for them and for companies to feel I was not trying to exploit them.'

Dassler kept the rights to FIFA's events, setting up a company he called ISL, part-owned by Adidas' Japanese partner Dentsu and run by his Adidas assistant Klaus Hempel, and Nally kept the rights for West Nally in athletic's first world championships in 1983 and their 1985 World Cup. ISL out-bid him two years later for the rights to the second championships. 'Our presentation was the most sophisticated and meaningful but we didn't get it because Horst was offering a vast sum up front.'

Guarantees can get out of control in sport. The IAAF have requested $60 million from ISL for the third championships and FIFA turned away an offer of 85 million Swiss francs for the 1994 World Cup from the Monaco-based agency Telemundi. Havelange had rewarded Dassler's original support by promising him, before he died in March, 1987, that ISL would have all advertising and marketing rights for the 1994 and 1998 World Cups. Nally says: 'They still might not make a profit but then that was never Horst's concern.'

'Horst was sport's godfather, the puppet master. But he's gone and there will be no puff of smoke and a replacement. He was a one-off, and his legacy to sport was to buy them back control of what was theirs, their right to sell their own events. He's given them tremendous power, enormous sums of money, large staffs. But at the same time he's removed the need for companies like ISL. The federations can do it themselves now. They have the rights, the experience, and now they can employ the professionals themselves.'

In October, 1986, Nally joined forces with Mike Luckwell, who had sold his interest in another media group for £25 million, changing West Nally's name to Parallel Media with the objective of restructuring it as a more broadly-based communications company including a television sports satellite channel. Within six months, they had agreed to part. 'They didn't have my interest or my feeling for sport, ' Nally explains.

Instead he took the rights he still owned in all the major European athletics events, the 1990 Commonwealth Games and the World Games to a deal with WCRS to become their international sponsorship arm. It teamed him with another successful British sports marketing agent, Alan Pascoe, a former Olympic athlete, who had sold his own company into WRCS as its domestic sponsorship division a year earlier.

'Everything on the sports marketing front has become very samey. All the proposals to companies are the same: name on the event, so many tickets, hospitality, sitings of advertising boards. Twenty years ago that was new. Now we have to lift it again. The sponsorship agency of the future must be a WCRS, large enough to look at the totality of a sporting event as any ad. agency does a media campaign, executing opportunities at every level.'

Even sport, he fears, may be losing its excitement. 'It's always been instant entertainment, instant drama; the ending always in doubt. There's no soap opera like it. But if there is too much of it, too many athletics meetings, too many tennis tournaments, too many pointless exhibitions, the excitement will go, and TV will go with it. Sport must keep itself fresh.'

Nally has seen fortunes pass through his hands but never bothered much about making one. 'I was always very cavalier about money. It was way down the list of my priorities. I wanted to be an innovator; gambling, creating something new which gave me a buzz, a creative director. I never wanted a fortune for doing that.'

The publishers would like to thank the following organizations and individuals for permission to use their photographs in this book: The International Olympic Committee, KBH Communications, Beecham Bovril Brands, Coca-Cola Great Britain, The Press Association, Tottenham Hotspur Football Club, Bob Woolf Associates Inc, Williams Grand Prix Engineering Ltd, Gallaher Ltd, Pascoe Nally International.